global marshall plan ( ) planetary contract

Global Marshall Plan

A Planetary Contract

For A Worldwide Eco-Social Market Economy

Franz Josef Radermacher
Global Marshall Plan Initiative (ed.)

07/2004

global marshall plan ( ) planetary contract

Imprint

Author	Franz Josef Radermacher in cooperation with Global Contract Foundation, Global Marshall Plan Foundation, Club of Budapest, Club of Rome, Eco-Social Forum Europe, Global Society Dialogue
Editor	Global Marshall Plan Foundation © July 2004 Global Marshall Plan Initiative, Hamburg
ISBN	3-9809723-0-5
Lectorship	Gudrun Gusel (freelance translator, graduated interpreter)
Translation	Bettina Hofstaetter
Coverpicture	Eco-Social Forum Europe
Coverconcept	Mark Müller-Bremer, rebranding
Layout	Katharina Peisker, Katja Pfeiffer
Composition	Helge Bork, Andrea von Lehmden, Markus Neuhoff, Maike Sippel, Sabine Stoeck
Financing	Global Marshall Plan Foundation
Printing	Ebner & Spiegel GmbH, CPI Books

Distribution
Global Marshall Plan Initiative
Rissener Landstrasse 193
22559 Hamburg, Germany
+49(0)40-822 90 420 (phone)
+49(0)40-822 90 421 (fax)
info@globalmarshallplan.org
www.globalmarshallplan.org

HRH Prince El Hassan bin Talal
President of the Club of Rome

Preface to the Global Marshall Plan Initiative

It is a fact that almost one half of the world's population is suffering from poverty. Poverty constitutes a main threat to peace and stability in our 'global village'. Furthermore, the extensive use of resources as we see it today causes serious environmental problems and endangers the habitat of future generations.

Regarding these problems, ambitious goals have been agreed upon internationally in the Millennium Development Declaration in 2000. However, respective efforts and concrete measures to bridge the divide between the rich and the poor, between North and South, and action to safeguard the environment have proved to be grossly inadequate.

The Global Marshall Plan Initiative seeks an international order based on partnership and cooperation. This should lead to an optimal use of human and natural resources to the benefit of all. The Initiative thus offers a viable comprehensive concept for stimulating a worldwide socio-economic development aiming at overcoming poverty. Furthermore, it provides a path of sustainability in the ecological field, taking into account the finiteness of natural resources on our planet by promoting and rewarding resource-efficient technologies and lifestyles.

I fully endorse the Global Marshall Plan Initiative which has been born out of the Club of Rome's spirit. As early as November 2003 I was able to present the concept of the Global Marshall Plan to the 3rd Environmental Forum in Magdeburg organized by UNEP and DaimlerChrysler. As I was able to see in Magdeburg and elsewhere, the Initiative hits the spirit of the time and has rapidly found widespread support. Our Club of Rome colleague Franz Josef Radermacher has contributed substantially to the message with his energetic and inspiring activities.

The Club of Rome and many of our individual members support the Global Marshall Plan Initiative, too. It is fully in line with our philosophy and offers a realistic perspective for the substantial changes required today. I strongly wish this publication inspires its readers to join the efforts of the Global Marshall Plan Initiative, thereby contributing towards a sustainable future for humankind!

HRH Prince El Hassan bin Talal
President, Club of Rome

His Royal Highness Prince El Hassan bin Talal of Jordan is committed to several international organizations and committees. Some he founded and initiated himself. His Royal Highness is inter alia President of the Club of Rome, and he is a moderator of the World Conference on Religions and Peace. Furthermore, His Royal Highness founded the Arab Thought Forum (1981) and the Parliament of Cultures (2002). Prince El Hassan is particularly concerned with the dialogue among different cultures and religions in order to obtain peace on the globe.

Josef Riegler
President, Eco-Social Forum

The "Global Marshall Plan Initiative - for a world-wide Eco-Social Market Economy" is, in my opinion, a concept which is well designed and well thought out. It offers the biggest chances to lead humankind to a good, sustainable and peaceful future, as opposed to the common one-sided and short-term solutions. This Initiative shows a way out of the "dead-end street" of the deadlocked global negotiations as well as the spiral of hatred and violence.
Franz Josef Radermacher is the "brain" behind the model for a sustainable world presented in this book. I consider it a special gift in my professional and political life that we met.

The "Global Marshall Plan" project, in connection with the order political model of an Eco-Social Market Economy, offers a unique symbiosis:

- Through a completely new form of financing - minimal levies on global capital transfers and global trade - the funds could be raised to finance the ambitious goals of the world community of states (Millennium Round Table), without increased burdening the national budgets or distorting economic competition. Consumers will hardly notice the proposed ways of financing, since normal price fluctuation account for a multiple of that. Fulfilling the necessary preconditions on the part of the receiving countries as well as mobilizing expert knowledge in development cooperation from experienced organizations, coordinated by the UN, raise the hope that the additional financial means will lead to the best possible result, namely humane living conditions for all men.

- The second strategic approach of the "Global Marshall Plan - for a worldwide Eco-Social Market Economy" project marks a fundamental distinction between our Initiative and other projects: through offering partnership in fair development cooperation, the "third world" countries shall be able to agree to the introduction of ecological and social standards, without worrying about competitive disadvantages.

- "Worldwide Eco-Social Market Economy" means that in all important global institutions and contracts (World Trade Organisation, International Monetary Fund, World Bank, International Labour Organisation, UN Environmental Program) the same ecological, social and procedural standards are introduced on a mandatory basis. This offers the opportunity for a functioning global governance concept, supported by the already existing organisations.

I thank Franz Josef Radermacher with all my heart for his ground-breaking initiatives. May this book contribute to mobilizing as many of the civil society's positive forces for this Initiative as possible.
I wish and hope that the EU will make this project its core concern, and that the EU will lead it to success, in cooperation with the developing countries, with the US and the global institutions, so that worldwide justice, sustainability and peace will get a chance.

Josef Riegler
President, Eco-Social Forum Europe
Former Vice Chancellor of Austria

Josef Riegler began his political career in 1972 and specialized in the field of agrarian economy. Since 1982 he has been the director of several agricultural organizations. In 1983 he became a member of the Austrian National Council. In 1987 he became Federal Minister for Agriculture and in 1989 he was elected Vice Chancellor. At present Josef Riegler is director of the Eco-Social Forum Europe, based in Austria.

Uwe Möller
Secretary General of the Club of Rome

There is nothing more powerful than an idea whose time has come.

Victor Hugo

The idea of a worldwide Marshall Plan is not new. The concept has already been promoted for a decade by personalities from a variety of backgrounds such as Franz Alt, Kofi Annan, Al Gore, Hans Küng, Susan George, Mikhail Gorbachev, HRH Prince El Hassan of Jordan, George Soros, Lutz Wicke, Georg Winter, and many more.

On May 16th, 2003, 16 politicians and representatives from non-governmental organizations and business associations met in Frankfurt to start the Global Marshall Plan Initiative. This circle gave mandates to Franz Josef Radermacher for the scientific coordination and to the Global Contract Foundation for the organizational coordination of the Initiative to be started.

The Initiative's long-term objective is to realize a worldwide Eco-Social Market Economy. An important and concrete first step in this direction is to attain the Millennium Development Goals by 2015, the Initiative's mid-term goal. The Initiative sees the European Union as the natural supporter of its concept in international politics.

Therefore, the short-term goal is to establish an advisory body within the EU on this issue in winter 2004/2005.

The deliberate, comprehensive strategy, on which the book at hand further elaborates, and the integration of a quickly growing number of relevant political, civil and private stakeholders - representatives of organizations ranging from Attac to DaimlerChrysler join in one initiative! - is the source of the great potential of the Global Marshall Plan Initiative.

This book contains the current status of contributions to the concept and strategy of the Global Marshall Plan Initiative. It has been developed in close interaction with the formulation of a basic position of the Initiative, published in parallel by Möller, Radermacher, Riegler, Soekader and Spiegel [70]. Its making was an open and integrative process which started at the Protestant Academy Tutzing in November 2003. Up to now, contributions and feedback from more than 50 experts have been incorporated into this text, and we would like this process to continue.

This book builds a starting point for a discussion process on a detailed, technical level, in which all societal groups from all over the world are cordially invited to participate. Many partner organizations of the Global Marshall Plan Initiative have already invited experts and stakeholders to join and enrich one of these forthcoming discussion forums, some of which are listed below.

- AIESEC International Congress, 23 August 2004, Hanover
- College des Ingenieurs, 8. and 15. September 2004, Paris
- Junior Chamber Germany, 22 September 2004, Paulskirche, Frankfurt
- Federation of Austrian Industry and GlobArt, 30 September 2004, Vienna
- GEXSI and Earth 3000, 8-9 October 2004, Bieberstein Forum, Dresden
- Club of Rome, 13-14 October 2004, Haus Rissen, Hamburg
- Eco-Social Forum Croatia, 21–22 October 2004, Zagreb
- European Baha'i Business Forum, 26 October 2004, Brussles
- Protestant Academy Tutzing, 31 October to 1 November 2004, Tutzing
- Foundation Osinga-Ages in November 2004 in Brussles
- UnternehmensGrün 17 November 2004, Stuttgart
- Consilium Conferentiarum Episcoporum Europae, Brussels, Autumn 2004
- OIKOS, January 2005, St. Gallen
- Representation of the State of Baden-Wuerttemberg in Brussels, Winter 2004, Brussels
- Presentation to the Delta State, Lagos, January 2005
- Geneva Group for Peace and Justice, February 2005, Geneva

- Junior Chamber Deggendorf, beginning of 2005, Deggendorf
- Umweltdachverband, Eco-Social Forum Europe and Institute for Environment, Peace and Development, beginning of 2005, Vienna
- Welthaus Innsbruck and Haus der Begegnung, beginning of 2005, Innsbruck
- Federal Association for Business Promotion and Foreign Trade, Friedrichsruh Castle, beginning of 2005
- Hauptkirche St. Katharinen 15 to 17 April 2005, Hamburg

Please contact us if you would like to organize a forum yourself.

The discussion process, which is to lead to an advanced and better defined version of the Global Marshall Plan concept, can also be tracked online at www.globalmarshallplan.org. Its results will be published as a revised version of the present book. The concept will then be used as a complementary means to concertedly address decision-makers on the European level.

Global Marshall Plan Initiative: Agenda

Winter 2004/2005
Start of a lobbying campaign with European decision-makers such as the European Parliament, the EU Commission, the Council of Europe, as well as national Governments and Parliaments for the establishment of a corresponding advisory body within the EU.

Summer / Autumn 2005
Advisory body is established and prepares a report on how the EU should promote a Global Marshall Plan.

2006
Worldwide consensus on a Global Marshall Plan is reached.

2007
A Global Marshall Plan is adopted at the date of Rio+15. Relevant international organizations and actors make preparations for implementation.

2008 – 2015
Implementation.

Politicians, entrepreneurs, representatives of civil society, inter-governmental organizations, science and culture as well as individuals - you are all cordially invited to join and advance the Initiative. The basic structure of the Initiative is an open matrix that builds upon subject-specific groups and sector-specific families on both national and international levels. This very structure allows a multitude of related activities to be decentrally coordinated in an efficient manner. Individual teams work proactively, according to the principle of "small but forceful units". They develop targeted strategies and independently implement them to maximize support for the Global Marshall

Plan Initiative in their respective target group. The following image may give you a slight impression of the matrix.
The organizational coordinator of the Initiative, the Global Contract Foundation with its President Frithjof Finkbeiner, has established a coordination office in Hamburg. Five young professionals, supported by a changing number of interns, coordinate the Initiative's activities. Interested people and participants of the Initiative are informed about current developments by the weekly info mail "(o) info" or the monthly newsletter "(o) news". Furthermore, the Initiative's website (www.globalmarshallplan.org) reflects the organizational matrix structure, leading visitors to the specific branch of the website which is managed by the respective coordinator of the team they would probably belong to.

What would the small man on the cover of this book do if the rock next to him lost its balance? If a hyper-system like today-'s world order steers in a wrong, not sustainable direction, the individual cannot do much about it. Yet if we form alliances with other positive forces on our globe from civil society, science, politics and the business sector, we can achieve a lot together. The Global Marshall Plan Initiative offers manyfold possibilities for each of us to get involved. What could you do?

- Give us feedback and share your ideas on how to improve the Initiative.
- Distribute this book and flyers about the Initiative. Both can be ordered through the Initiative's website. You can also advise other interested people to order a copy of the book.
- Spread the word within your professional and private networks. Get your friends, neighbors, classmates and colleagues to join the Global Marshall Plan Initiative, and help us further expanding our global network.

- Contact your government. Call or write to your elected representatives on regional, national and European levels and introduce to them the concept of the Global Marshall Plan Initiative.
- Inform the media. When you find related news articles on the issues touched by the Global Marshall Plan, write letters to the responsible journalists.
- Organize a public event. You can organize an event in your community and bring people together around these concerns:
  - Organize a discussion forum (Discuss the Global Marshall Plan), for further information please contact our coordination office (info@globalmarshallplan.org or +49(0)40-82290420).
- Become a representative / multiplier in your country or field of expertise:
  - Identify key-players / organizations.
  - Lobby with parliamentarians and other decision makers.
- Become actively involved in one of our teams (see matrix).
- Help with translations.
- Raise funds. Fundraising is a great way to support the Global Marshall Plan Initiative, as well as to raise awareness and bring in new supporters.
- Make a donation, for example via the credit card tool on our website (www.globalmarshallplan.org).

- Become a partner of the Global Marshall Plan Initiative through regular substantial, material or financial contribution.
- Participate in our online forums (www.globalmarshallplan.org/forum).
- Place a link to the Global Marshall Plan website on your own website. A toolkit is available on the Global Marshall Plan website (www.globalmarshallplan.org).
- And more...
  There are many more steps you can take to support the Initiative. Your creativity is the only limit to effective action. The more people know about the Global Marshall Plan, the greater the chance that we will reach our short-term goal of an EU advisory body - and further goals. Please keep the Global Marshall Plan Initiative posted on your agenda.

You must be the change you wish to see in the world.

Mahatma Gandhi

Uwe Möller
Secretary General of the Club of Rome

Uwe Möller was born in 1935 in Hamburg. From 1955 to 1959 he studied economics at Hamburg University. Since 1960 he was member of staff and from 1983 to 1999 director of Haus RISSEN, International Institute for Politics and Economics. Since January 1999 Secretary General of the Club of Rome.

Global Marshall Plan - Strategy, Structure (draft)

(coordinators may be interim coordinators, subject to change)

		international	Europe													Americas			Africa			...
			Austria	Belgium	Croatia	Finnland	Germany	Huungary	Italy	Portugal	Russia	Slovenia	Sweden	Switzerland	...	Mexico	USA	...	Mozambique	Nigeria	South Africa	...
National Coordinators			Riegler		Baotic	Kalimo	Finkbeiner	Györi-Nagy	Burger	Schmidt	Kapitza	Socan	Wijkman	Sutsch		Neugebauer	Mesarovics Lehrheuer		Madjera		Madjera	
Subject Groups																						
	Contents	Radermacher																				
	Editing Team	Soekadar																				
	Coordination	Finkbeiner																				
	PR Communication	Boehncke / Henschel																				
	...																					
Families																						
public	European Commission																					
	European Parliament			Allen																		
	Council of Europe																					
	National Parliaments																					
	Political "Global Players"																					
	Cities and local authorities																					
	Regional Policy																					
	...																					
private	Agriculture																					
	Business associations	Härthe																				
	Chambers of commerce																					
	Global players																					
	Small and medium-sized enterprises																					
	World Economic Forum																					
	...																					

civil	Authors, Intellectuals	Spiegel																					
	Catholic church						Steinke																
	Challenged people																						
	Creators and promoters of culture	A. Möller																					
	Education and academia	Ferger					Gansczyk																
	Environmental organizations																						
	Gender / women																						
	Health																						
	Human rights groups																						
	Implementation	Koch-Weser																					
	Indigenous people																						
	Law																						
	Other churches / religious groups																						
	Philanthrophic organizations																						
	Protestant church						Dettweiler																
	Science and technology community																						
	Service Clubs (Rotary, Lions, ...)																						
	Social movement	Hesse																	Akarue				
	Sports																						
	Students	Herrmann		Bauchmüller			Guller																
	...																						
intergovern mental	IMF																						
	UN																						
	UNCTAD																						
	UNDP	Pralong																					
	UNEP																						
	UNESCO																						
	UNFCCC																						
	World Bank																						
	WTO																						
	...																						
liaison offices	Brussels	Häringer																					
	Geneva	Ergas																					
	...																						

Dr. Maritta R. von Bieberstein Koch-Weser

The path is the goal.
The "Global Marshall Plan" is on the right path.

This book reflects the search for new beginnings, true breakthroughs, and new social organization models that can make these possible. It is the document of an emerging movement, the expression of an energetic impulse into the only direction that could restore world peace mid-term, and better retain peace in the long-term.

The world is too unjust. Chances of survival and access to things that make life humane are unequally distributed, as the Human Development Report of the UNDP shows every year. Two billion humans, a third of humankind, live below the so-called subsistence level. About 30 million children die annually before the age of five, simply because they do not have access to clean drinking water and hygienic surroundings. "Sustainability" and intergenerational justice are on the lips and in the wishful thinking of many, but implementation on a grand scale is missing.

The merit of this book is the search for concepts, new instruments, and concrete ways that could make a substantial improvement in the 21st century. This search does not begin at zero. On the contrary, it can draw from six decades of experience. The world tried "progress" and the basic approaches of development, and learned from them. There is a foundation of successful technical and social beginnings established. However, the means to extensively replicate their adoption are missing beyond the drop in the ocean.

Chances are great that the transcendence of the parched foreign aid could bring about change:

- Social entrepreneurs, individuals and organizations, and also many governments have, over the years, learned how to make advancements in education and health systems and make effective use of natural resources.

- Corporations also partially entered the team of the social businesses, locally and also globally, e.g. with their support of educational campaigns (e.g. "Overcoming the Digital Divide") or programs for the fight against HIV/Aids.

- Technologies in energy, water and sanitation infrastructure have become cheaper and more intelligent and make a decentralized, local model of progress possible.

- Thanks to the communications revolution, education, which apart from health is the most important element in increasing the standards of living, can tear down boundaries. Through access to municipal computers, television sets, videos in schools, children in slums and remote rural areas can learn even in places where teachers are rare or poorly trained.

- Social investment in developing countries could become a standard element of investment funds and financial assets. Meanwhile competent investment advice is offered for social investment in developing countries, e.g. by the Global Exchange for Social Investment, ACCESS, or Global Giving.

Nothing would be more false to say than there is no "absorptive capacity" in order to implement a Global Marshall Plan and the United Nations Millennium Development Goals. If the Global Marshall Plan were to come to realization, it could be supported by and rely on a network of expertise and experience.

The problem is that there are solutions but just not enough of them. We have to become more ambitious and by far more impatient. And here is where money plays an indespensable and essential role.

We must come to a point where money serves humans and peace, not the defense industry. On the one hand US$ 900 billion are spent annually on defense and another US$ 300 billion on agricultural subsidies that have explicitly negative effects on developing countries, on the other hand there is a shameful 50 billion dollars of development aid worldwide - a sum which has been stagnating for years.

We need systematic, large-scale, ambitiously scheduled approaches that equally distribute chances for a humane life. May this book impart urgency and motivate many people to work towards a programmatic advancement.

Dr. Maritta Koch-Weser
President, Earth3000
CEO GEXSI

Maritta R. von Bieberstein Koch-Weser is founder and chairperson of Earth3000, an international non-profit organization situated in Berlin. Before that, she was CEO of the IUCN - The World Conservation Union. From 1980 to 1998 Ms Koch-Weser was employed by the World Bank, and was in charge of the development of environmental and social programs. Currently, she is the CEO of the Global Exchange for Social Investment (GEXSI) which promotes social investment and the mobilization of financial resources.

Jane Roberts
34 Million Friends

Comments from a Grassroot on the Global Marshall Plan / Planetary Contract

I have been asked to comment on the Global Marshall Plan Initiative. My perspective on this is a little different because I am a grassroot, which means in English someone who, while no expert, strives to make change by enlisting the help of normal everyday citizens.

In the United States I am cofounder of a two year long movement called 34 Million Friends of the United Nations Population Fund. Our government under President Bush has refused to release the $34 million that Congress has voted every year for UNFPA. Lois Abraham and I started asking 34 million Americans to contribute one dollar. The results are promising (www.UNFPA.org and/or www.34millionfriends.org) and we have momentum.

After our first $1 million came in, UNFPA decided to encourage Europeans to take part, not to make up for the US default but to give ordinary citizens in the EU a chance to say to the world that women's lives, reproductive health, and family planning choices should be a top priority of governments. There was a gala event at the Residence Palace in Brussels on May 7, 2003. The following evening I talked about this initiative to the Club of Rome at the invitation of Raoul Weiler. It is through this connection that I made email acquaintance with Professor Radermacher. I was invited to take part in planning meetings for the Global Marshall Plan but was unable to attend due to speaking engagements in the US.

Professor Radermacher sent me his book, "Balance or Destruction: Ecosocial Market Economy as the Key to Global

Sustainable Development". In Chapter 18 he talks about human numbers, the "youth bulge" on the planet today being a reason for the probable 8 billion human beings by the year 2030. A trend toward increased urbanization with the world's mega-cities even now incapable of keeping up with needed infrastructure, schools, sanitation, transportation etc. is presented as perhaps an intractable long term problem. He offers the insight that perhaps the US lack of support for global population efforts and its religious stand against humane legal abortion is a way of perpetuating poverty and strengthening a system of an asymmetrical grasp for the earth's resources. I had not thought in such cynical terms, but may start to.

He retakes up this theme again on page 215 talking about the blocking of funds by the Bush administration for the United Nations Population Fund. "Reactionary religious forces in the USA are asserting their influence on the government and by the withdrawal of financial support for measures in regard to family planning and reproductive health are perpetuating indescribable misery for hundreds of thousands of women, children, and families in this world, including unnecessary deaths by the thousands." How true!

In my view, when the world takes care of women, women take care of the world. The world is doing a terrible job. In 1994, in Cairo, Egypt, the International Conference on Population and Development (ICPD) adopted a 20 year Program of Action which included four main components, universal literacy (two-thirds of the world's illiterate are women) opening civil society to all equally, reducing infant and child mortality to the lowest possible number, and most important, making knowledge about and affordable access to reproductive health and family planning universally available. Abortion was not to be considered a method of family planning. (The world might not, but women do, to the tune of 40 per minute in poor countries because family planning isn't available).

The cost of adopting this agenda was to range between $17 and $21 billion per year with the target countries paying two thirds and the donor countries one third. The target countries have furnished about 75 percent of what they promised. The donor countries have furnished less than one half of what they promised with the US at the bottom.

In conclusion I would say let us first live up to the very letter of the Cairo agreement. Nothing could equal in importance the education health, and equality of the world's women. They are the key, I think, to sustainable development, to population stabilization, to environmental and human health. They are the key also to worldwide peace and stability. Embracing women in all aspects of life has really never been tried in any concentrated fashion. The Global Marshall Plan if it embraces the women of the world will be a marvelous contribution to the world and to civilized dialog about the future of people, the planet, and the generations to come. I know Professor Radermacher feels as deeply as I do about this and will be a wonderful voice for change.

Jane Roberts,
34 Million Friends

Jane Roberts was born in 1941 in San Diego, California. For 30 years she has been focusing on women's issues, reproductive health, and international family planning. When the US administration decided to defund UNFPA, she started the 34 million friends of UNFPA-campaign.
see www.34millionfriends.org

Prof. Dr. Ram Adhar Mall

The Global Marshall Plan Initiative from the point of view of Intercultural Philosophy

The Global Marshall Plan / Planetary Contract Initiative for a worldwide Eco-Social Market Economy aims at winning business, civil society and politics for a new era of cooperation to create global security, peace and wealth for everyone, as well as ecological sustainability. The Initiative feels indebted to Kofi Annan's "Dialogue Among Civilizations - Crossing the Divide" for global sustainable co-existence in the new century. It is therefore based on intercultural humanism as its worldview and "world ethos" as moral minimal consensus. The latter is complemented through the "Earth Charta" with its emphasis on sustainability. Intercultural humanism, world ethos and Earth Charta are also, as an overlapping of different cultures, supported and critically accompanied by intercultural philosophy.

The young branch of research of intercultural philosophy gained importance through globalisation and the end of the Cold War. Philosophers from Europe, the US, Latin America, India, China, Japan and Africa, as well as the Arab League are involved in this field. It emanates from the perception that there is an increasing cross-cultural integration of the world community under scientific, economic and financial aspects, as well as aspects of transportation and communication. This is in contrast to the co-existing and often conflicting grown societal, political, religious and philosophical structures of the individual cultures. This contrast is the challenge for intercultural philosophy. It decided to clear the respective cultural heritage of the individual cultures and to promote the dialogue between cultures from an intercultural aspect. This shall be achieved by forming a theoretical and practical basis for the encounter of different cultures, religions and philosophies. The intercultural understanding linked with this dialogue is considered by intercultural philosophy as the philosophical contribution to reaching the idea of all peoples living together in harmony. The alternative to this idea, as described in Huntington's "Clash of Civilisations", threatens the mere existence of mankind. Thus intercultural philosophy is the philosophical precursor of the manifest "Crossing the Divide".

Intercultural philosophy is the name of an attitude, which wants to be a way of thinking, as well as way of living. It focuses on the respective historically grown forms of thinking and shaping, as well as the various patterns of interpretation and understanding in their cultural diversity. Intercultural communication has to be led by the attitude that "truth" does not belong to any political system, neither intra-culturally nor inter-culturally. Intercultural philosophy therefore rejects all tendencies of absolutation of any meta physics, religion, culture, political world view, logic, or ethics. In this way it attempts to counter the "truth-fanaticism" of fundamentalist currents which are always linked with a claim for truth and can occur in many disguises, e.g. economic fundamentalism. They counter it with epistemic, methodological, metaphysical, ethic-moral and even religious-philosophical modesty in their interaction with traditional worldviews.

Intercultural philosophy especially addresses any reductive hermeneutics, which does not try to understand something foreign, but adapts it to their own ways of understanding and therewith changes or even dominates it. In contrast to reductive hermeneutics, intercultural hermeneutics avoids a metaphysical preliminary decision concerning the question of truth and focuses on the symmetrical approach of "wanting to understand" and "wanting to be understood". It is the task of a philosophy comparing culture to analyse the ethics of different cultures with their patterns of argument, their forms of ethos and moral views in a dialogue of cultures with respect to their common ground and the differences. The task could also be to promote the common ground with the long-term objective of realising the moral claim of good cohabitation of the different cultures, which is also expressed in the manifest "Dialogue Among Civilizations - Crossing the Divide".

Part of clearing the respective historical heritage of different cultures, apart from the clarification of perceptions of the relations between humans, is also the clarification of the perception of the relations of humans to nature and to the universe. Modern man does not like the Greek, Chinese, Indian or Native American relatedness with the cosmos, because it dictates man's and history's course of emergence and decay. The scientific-technical control over nature, which in an anthropocentric delusion of interests, did not respect sufficiently the interests of the variety of life. Modern made man forget that nature can exist without man but man cannot exist without nature. The consequences of anthropocentric ruthlessness, beats back on humankind in the form of an endangerment of the world climate, the loss of biodiversity and other threats to the complex ecological balance. Intercultural philosophy highly respects what natural sciences and technology have achieved, but in the same way respects the wisdom of other cultures and therefore rejects the command over nature in form of exploitation and plundering to the detriment of future human generations and other creatures as an anthropocentric aberration.

The wisdom of the philosophies of the world's cultures could contribute to a way out of the problems by urging people to overcome the often dominating ego-centrism, ethno-centrism, but also the anthropocentrisms and to apprehend that man is embedded in nature and to let this be the guiding principle. Neither a crude "back to nature" nor an exclusive "back to culture" but a "back to nature taking the detour of culture" linked with the insight that this could lead to a sustainable co-existence for all creatures in one big community of cosmic nature on our common home planet, the Earth.

The Initiative for a Global Marshall Plan / planetary contract tries to win the powerful designers of globalisation: the financial world, the private enterprise and politics for such a sustainable co-existence oriented towards global justice, sustainability and peace by peaceful means. Orientation towards global justice can lead to overcoming hunger, poverty and diseases and can lay the foundations for a satisfying life in cultural diversity. Orientation towards sustainability shows responsibility for future generations and aspires a harmonic life in line with nature. After the most cruel century in human history, in which way too often violent dominance over man and nature was executed, realising justice and sustainability could enhance the chances for peace through peaceful means in and with nature in the new century which so far has been just as cruel. Therefore, the Global Marshall Plan / planetary contract Initiative deserves our support.

Prof. Dr. Ram Adhar Mall,
Native of India, building bridges between Asian and European Culture
Founding president Society of Intercultural Philosophy

Klaudius Gansczyk
Society of Intercultural Philosophy
Coordinator Global Marshall Plan Education Family

Ram Adhar Mall was born in India. He graduated with degrees in psychology, philosophy, Sanskrit, English language and literature from the University of Economy in Kalkutta. After finishing his PhD in 1963 in Germany, he returned to India to lecture at the Jadavpur University in Kalkutta. In 1991 Prof. Mall was elected President of the Society of Intercultural Philosophy. Since 1998 he is professor at the University of Munich for intercultural philosophy.

In memoriam Robert Pestel

This work is dedicated to the memory of Robert Pestel who died on April 18, 2003. Robert Pestel was an unwavering fighter for a better future. Continuing the work of his father, Eduard Pestel, and acting in the tradition of the Club of Rome's work and thinking, he dealt with the problems of the globe and how to organize a better future for the whole world and its people. He used system theory models to get a better feeling for the dynamics of development and innovation processes, and he networked with hundreds of people around the globe in a most intensive way. He was very persevering in following his visions and had an unbelievable energy until the end.

Within the European Commission he shaped the thinking about sustainability, its economic, social, cultural and ecological aspects, and the correspondence to a global contract. He also understood the power of the Internet and other communication networks for good and ill, he was an engineer who took the rebound effect into account, and he was always active to make civil society take on a bigger role and more responsibility in shaping the world's future. Making the best use of the power of insight, networking and communication was one of his biggest hopes. Consequently, he believed in the value of information and open debate. Concerning communication, he was willing to involve science and formal argumentation systems as much as subsymbolic approaches, a reference to emotions and reflections via different forms of art.

This work is inspired and shaped throughout by his thinking, visions and support. He was a great friend and co-worker, initiated many projects, achieved a lot, and fought until his final hours when he was taken away from us much too soon. He was a great person. We miss him.

Robert Pestel

European Commission, Brussels
German Association for the Club of Rome
Brussels EU-Chapter of the Club of Rome
Collaboration on the Second World Model of the Club of Rome,
Member of the Advisory Council of the website Deutschland.de

Global Marshall Plan

A Planetary Contract

For A Worldwide
Eco-Social Market Economy

Franz Josef Radermacher
Global Marshall Plan Initiative

07/2004

Abstract

The text at hand provides considerations on a **Global Marshall Plan** in terms of a **Planetary Contract**, i.e. in response to the difficult situation of world politics at the beginning of the new century. This Contract is intended as a step towards a global **Eco-Social Market Economy**, which we regard as an attractive win-win alternative in compliance with the idea of a sustainable development, versus the extensively unregulated globalization processes prevalent today.

As concrete target to be implemented until 2015, the Initiative adopts the **UN Millennium Development Goals.** Today, reaching these targets seems rather unlikely, unless the worldwide community introduces decisive efforts. In order to achieve these goals, international agreements are needed. Requirements include the **further opening of markets**, as well as **additional funds** for development cooperation; the latter have already been identified.

Through new forms of international cooperation, these funds are applicative for investment in: the **promotion of international development**, the elimination of poverty and hardship, the promotion of cultural exchange, and the protection of the environment. This requires in particular that NGOs and representatives of global civil society are given a stronger stake in this process than they have today.

We suggest that central standards of the International Labor Organization (ILO), standards of UNESCO, and major environmental agreements are combined with the WTO regime and the IWF and WB, to serve as an international economic framework for appropriate support programs. This would constitute a vital step towards a worldwide **Eco-Social Market Economy.**

Simultaneously, the paper delineates clear perspectives on how to achieve our goals, a timetable and, most importantly, suggestions concerning the raising of the necessary funds. In 2008-2015, the additional international investment in boosting development should amount to approximately **US$ 105 billion per year**, in accordance with UN studies on the issue.

Kofi Annan
UN Secretary General's Message for New Year 2004
[5]

Dear Peoples of the United Nations,

Your Organization, which I have the honour to serve, has just been through one of the hardest years in its history.

We have seen war in Iraq and deep divisions among nations, about grave issues of war and peace. On 19 August, in a bomb attack on our headquarters in Baghdad, we lost some of our best and most beloved colleagues.

These events have distracted the world's leaders from dealing with other threats – threats which, to most people, are more immediate and more real. I mean the threats of extreme poverty and hunger, unsafe drinking water, environmental degradation and endemic or infectious disease.

These dangers stalk large parts of our planet.
They kill millions and millions of people every year.
They destroy societies.
They fuel division and desperation.

After a year of war and division, it's time to focus more of our energy on people's health and welfare. It's time to make sure that poor countries have a real opportunity to develop. And it's time we took decisive action to save the resources of our planet.

Yes, we have to fight terrorism.
Yes, we must prevent the spread of deadly weapons.
But let's also say Yes to development.
Let's bring hope into the lives of those who suffer.
Without development and hope, there will be no peace.

Just over three years ago, at the Millennium Summit, leaders of all nations pledged to provide that hope. They set themselves precise, time-bound targets – the Millennium Development Goals. But in 2003 we did not live up to these promises. We let ourselves be swept along by the tide of war and division. 2004 must be different. It must be the year when we begin to turn the tide.

We can turn the tide against HIV/AIDS, if we act on the "three-by-five" initiative – the World Health Organization's plan to get three million people on anti-retroviral treatment by 2005. It's a bold target, but it can be met – if rich countries, poor and afflicted countries, governments, civil society, the private sector and the United Nations system all pull together – and if the Global Fund to Fight AIDS, Tuberculosis and Malaria is fully funded.

We can turn the tide against hunger, if we all work together to make existing food stocks available to hungry people everywhere, and to help Africa produce the extra food it needs.

And we can turn the tide in world trade, if governments do as they promised, and make the current round of negotiations a true "development round".

We don't need any more promises. We need to start keeping the promises we already made.

Let's all make that our New Year's resolution – and I wish you a very Happy New Year!

To meet these Goals would cost only a fraction of what our world spends on weapons of war. Yet it would bring hope to billions, and greater security to us all.

Introduction / Summary

Due to rapid globalization, our world is in a difficult situation. The New Year's Message from UN General Secretary **Kofi Annan** [5], printed at the beginning of this report, illustrates both the problem and the existing challenges. There are high growth rates worldwide, and innovations occur at a speed never observed before. Yet at the same time, the global situation regarding the state of the environment, poverty, and distribution issues is getting more and more unsustainable, as does the balance between cultures. Against this background, a group of sixteen NGOs started an initiative "Global Marshall Plan / Planetary Contract" in the summer of 2003. Conceived as a movement for world peace, sustainability, and equity (www.initiative-weltfrieden.org), the Initiative is targeted at changing this adverse situation [70]. The author is substantially involved in this process.

This text is designed as a report to the Initiative **Global Marshall Plan / Panetary Contract** and provides multifaceted considerations and materials to a broad audience. It could not have been accomplished in this form without the help of many concerned people, who offered their suggestions and substantial advice. In this respect, the text has partly the character of a **group effort**. The acknowledgements at the end of the document indicate many of the persons whose contributions were vital to the creation of this text.

Furthermore, it is supplemented by the systematic support from the team of the Global Contract Foundation's coordinating office in Hamburg (www.global-contract.org), which coordinates the activities of the Global Marshall Plan Initiative (www.globalmarshallplan.org). In this context, the author intends to continue studying all feedback to this text and to integrate it into the next revision of this report when a new print edition will be in planning.

The considerations outlined in this text have been inspired by, among others: the document "Crossing the Divide. A Dialogue Among Civilizations" initiated by **Kofi Annan** [3], **Mikhail Gorbachev's** "My Manifesto for the Earth" [34], **Al Gore's** "Earth in the Balance" [35], "World Ethos" by **Hans Küng** [62], the essays on human duties edited by **Helmut Schmidt** [100], and, last but not least, by the **Earth Charta** [117]. It also ties in with a dedicated initiative for an Ecologic Marshall Plan which was propagated by masterminds like **Franz Alt, Carlhanns Damm, Wolfgang Engelhardt, Joschka Fischer, Maximilian Gege, Jo Leinen, Eva Quistorp, Wolfgang Rauls**, and **Lutz Wicke** in 1997 and was able to collect approximately 750,000 signatures in favor of the proposed plans [2]. All of these comprehensive reflections and positions supplied central points of orientation and organizing principles for the setup of the Initiative for a **Global Marshall Plan / Planetary Contract.**

Where the concrete factual elaboration on a Global Marshall Plan as developed in the following is concerned (with the long-term objective of a **worldwide Eco-Social Market Economy**, the integration of existing global regimes as an approach to an institutional design and Global Governance, new international financing instruments and mechanisms of implementation), this text is a direct continuation of the reflections presented in [87] .

The Global Marshall Plan Initiative's core orientation has the following objective:

- Europe takes the lead in a worldwide movement for an eco-social Global Marshall Plan;
- It pursues the elaboration of a concept for the implementation and funding of such a plan;
- It adopts this as Europe's official position on all future world summits.

The intermediate goal is to convene an advisory board of the European Union, bringing together individuals from all divisions of society and all parts of the world to work on the elaboration of a consistent European proposal on this topic.

The plan discussed here aims to provide the already globalized economy with an **adequate worldwide regime** for the markets, promoting goals like world peace, equity, and sustainability. As regards the realization of sustainability demands, please refer to the analysis [127] of a task force installed by the UN Commission on Sustainable Development; for questions regarding the **equity between the generations**, to studies by various youth organizations [113, 114, 144]. The promotion of the stated goals, which also include the **establishment of transparency** [122] and the **clear assignment of responsibility**, is far from being a top priority in market development today, despite many statements to the contrary. Incidentally, these apparent shortcomings and the threats they pose have inspired extensive commitments from major companies on the questions raised here, in terms of, e.g., **Excellence** or **Leadership in Sustainability** and **Corporate Social Governance**. To mention but a few, on the international level there are **Global Compact** (www.un.org/News/Press/docs/1999/19990201.sgsm6881.html) induced by **Kofi Annan**, **World Business Council on Sustainable Development** (www.wbcsd.org), or, in Germany, **econsense** (www.econsense.de). As regards Corporate Social Responsibility, please refer to takingitglobal (www.takingitglobal.org/themes/csr).

The long-term objective behind the ideas presented here is an **Eco-Social Global Market Economy** [87, 93] in which markets and competition are inseparably linked to high standards - maybe development state dependent - regarding the welfare of all human beings. Such standards are also key instruments for the elimination of worldwide poverty. To implement them, it is crucial that the rich countries **open their markets further while taking co-financing measures** for the benefit of the developing countries, ultimately effectuating appropriate worldwide regimes. In return, the developing countries have to prove willing to implement accordant standards, in spite of the concomitant loss of some current competitive advantages. Thus, the objective is to implement a worldwide process adapted from the **EU enlargement process**, the **US Marshall Plan for Europe** after World War II, as well as the central demands voiced by developing countries at all World Summits of the last decades (idea of a **Planetary Contract**) [4, 20, 21, 22, 23, 30, 31, 32, 33, 82, 87, 93, 94, 124].

Today, such a contract for the entire world is pressing and overdue - particularly so with regard to the events of September 11, 2001, the questions raised by **current neo-imperial policy patterns**, recent devastations on global financial markets, the failure of the New Economy, mounting global environmental problems, as well as the explosive, ever more manifest collision of extreme exponents from different cultures, resulting from the **inadequate regulation of the globalization of economy**.

Against this background, the Global Marshall Plan Initiative's short-term objective is the installment of an advisory board by the European Union in 2004 with the intention to develop a corresponding position as **Europe's vision for the future of the globe** for future summits. Such a vision for the future can readily be linked with the **follow-up processes to the Rio and Johannesburg Summits**, with **Agenda 21** and the **European Strategy on Sustainability**.

The immediate goal of the Initiative Global Marshall Plan / Planetary Contract is the convention of an advisory board by the EU after the EU parliamentary elections in summer 2004 and the forming of the new EU Commission, with the intention to develop a respective position as Europe's vision for the future of the globe, to be represented at future World Summits.

A Global Marshall Plan / Planetary Contract is regarded as an intermediate step towards a worldwide Eco-Social Market Economy. The concrete goals pursued by the Initiative until 2015 are represented by the **United Nations Millennium**

Development Goals (www.un.org/millenniumgoals/), which can claim broad international consensus. Incorporated into our considerations are the statements of the recent, important **ILO Report** on the social dimension of globalization [47], as well as the EU strategy on sustainability and the UN activities in the wake of the WSSD in Johannesburg, 2002, and of WSIS in Geneva, 2003. Simultaneously, we actively observe the review process on the UN Millennium Development Goals, due 2005.

Positions regarding the financial requirements are based on an analysis of the United Nations (**Zedillo Report**, www.un.org/reports/financing/full_report.pdf), the very comprehensive European position by the British Chancellor of the Exchequer **Gordon Brown** [12] for the 2002 World Summit Rio+10 in Johannesburg (www.globalpolicy.org/socecon/ffd/2002/1216brown.htm), as well as this position's development in 2004 [13], studies by various UN bodies, and **George Soros**' analysis in his strive towards an Open Society (Open Society Initiatives, G. Soros, www.soros.org) [4, 20, 26, 27, 55, 66, 104, 105, 106, 107, 109, 118, 123, 124, 125, 126, 128]. The allocation of additional funds should coincide with **further opening of the rich countries' markets** to the rest of the world, most notably to the poorest countries, in a suitable manner.

As the first parliament, the **German Bundestag** has dealt with the challenges of globalization in-depth. The Enquete Commission **'Globalization of the World Economy - Challenges and Answers'** has in its final report (Bundestagsdrucksache 14/9200) taken up the results of international conferences and commissions, agreements and scientific theoretical approaches. It has given the parliament 200 recommendations for action on **how to design globalization**. Some of these were already made Acts of Parliament: fighting money laundering and corruption, integration of environmental and social standards, as well as the precautionary principle into the WTO's body of regulations and solutions for the issues of debt relief. Furthermore, there are recommendations made for reaching gender equality, fighting corruption, for a new order of competition, the establishment of an international insolvency order and **for a stronger participation of the civil society** and the parliaments in policy making (www.bundestag.de/gremien/welt/glob_end/). Chairperson of the Enquete was **Prof. Ernst Ulrich von Weizsäcker**, MP and member of the Club of Rome, who is closely linked to the Global Marshall Plan Initiative in his role as member of the board of trustees of the Global Contract Foundation.

Based on the above studies, an additional **US$ 980 billion** will be needed until 2015, on top of the current level of international development assistance. Moreover, these funds must be used following **distinctly different mechanisms than currently applied**, as will be illustrated. **The question of implementation is yet a bigger challenge than the raising of funds**. Because of commitments already undertaken by certain countries from the year 2006 on, this sum will be reduced to approximately US$ 860 billion. Under an adequate regime, and focusing on developing countries that are willing to cooperate in terms of the requirements to be met, these funds could be raised per annum from 2008 onwards by, e.g.:

1. **Special Drawing Rights** of the International Monetary Fund, starting approximately with US$ 30, then 40 billion in aid of the developing countries.

2. A worldwide tax on financial transactions (**Tobin tax**), at a level initially of 0.01%, then 0.02% of value traded. This should yield initially approximately US$ 30, then 40 billion in funds per annum.

3. A worldwide tax on trade (**Terra tax**), amounting initially to 0.35 %, then 0.5 % of internationally traded goods in the context of the WTO. This should yield initially approximately US$ 30, then 40 billion per annum.

Alternative approaches that in the author's view may be less practicable in the short run, and thus less likely to be agreed on, are e.g. (4) **direct governmental transfers** (in terms of effect, this could be realized at least partly along the lines of Special Drawing Rights (1), (5) **taxes on resource consumption and socially straining activities**, and (6) a **fair trade on rights for the access to and pollution of resources**. Other alternatives aim at appropriate **endowment funds, bonds**, etc. Finally, the idea of an **International Finance Facility** [13] was suggested by British Chancellor of the Exchequer Gordon Brown and subsequently taken up internationally.

An argument in favor of approach (4), as pursued by members of the EU, e.g., is that it avoids special strains on those value-added processes that are tightly linked to international trade and globalization. However, **George Soros**, highly adept with global finance markets, points out very persuasively in [109] that particularly in this area new value-added potentials have evolved with highly asymmetrical means of access, indicating in fact a special justification for this approach.

Concerning a Tobin tax [24, 120] it must be noted that the usual counter-arguments against such a tax do not apply in the context pursued here [8, 138]. The proposition at hand does not (primarily) aim at effectively obstructing or penalizing speculation on financial markets, but much rather at **raising the means to promote worldwide development**.

At the same time, we do not advocate that Europe presses ahead. Rather, the topic is pursued solely in the context of a worldwide implementation. If the developed countries stand together, it will be no problem to force even **offshore banking locations** to comply by purely economic mechanisms. Steps towards a more stringent control and demands of accountability for such banking locations are being prepared internationally (albeit for different reasons), and are long overdue. Nevertheless, this point requires further textual analysis.

If on the basis of the alternatives described in this text, which represents merely an initial input for further considerations by panels yet to be convened, we are in favor of the funding mechanisms (1) to (3), this is for solely pragmatic reasons concerning their **implementability** within relatively short timeframes. A similar effect can be achieved with (1) and with (4). Also, (3) has similar effects to (5), at least to a certain degree. Finally and detached from what is said here, the approach addressed in (6) should play a role within the continuation of the agreements achieved in the **Kyoto Protocol** from 2012 on, e.g. in form of a **market- and incentive-orieted global climate certificate system** [87, 136, 137], and could eventually be linked to a **Global Marshall Plan / Planetary Contract**.

As important as the raising of funds for co-financing measures and further opening of markets by the rich countries, or even more so, are **new forms of implementation** [14, 17, 109, 145]. For such new approaches, the program could avail itself of, among others, the **World Bank** and the **United Nations Development Program**, as well as cooperate with **UNEP** and, for example, **UNESCO** and **United Nations Population Fund (UNFPA)**. On their part, these partners should rely on **local initiatives and NGOs** more than hitherto, support **small and medium-sized companies**, **adapted technologies** and **local efforts to increase value added and welfare**. Furthermore, they should elect **private development initiatives** applying for co-financing measures and support programs in competitive selection procedures controlled by an independent jury [109]. Many other ideas exist for this important sector, but there is still a lot to do. The **quality of any program is ultimately determined by how it is implemented**.

Concerning standards, the core **standards of the International Labour Organization ILO** (www.ilo.org/public/english/bureau/gender/newsite2002/standard/), UNEP recommendations, core directives of the **Global Environmental Agreements**, and UNESCO recommendations should be made binding in the context of the WTO, and possibly also when credits are granted by the International Monetary Fund and the World Bank [42, 87]. This takes up a demand for the advancement of the WTO that is often expressed by the developed world and especially the US, corresponding in particular to the concerns of unions in developed countries and to worldwide concerns of environmentalists.

At the same time, the **economic, social, and cultural human rights**, internationally binding since 1996, yet only marginally perceived in this form, could be made substantially binding [139].
From the author's point of view, the issue of the development of world population and the implementation of the **reproductive rights of all human beings** should also be addressed in this context [1, 18, 19, 51, 54, 80, 83].

A big challenge for the required process of integrating various international regimes will be the creation of a **legal institution on an international level** for the Global Governance System evolving from this integration of existing entities. In particular, this authority must appropriately integrate the **WTO's dispute settlement system, and possibly the respective elements within IWF and World Bank**, in order to make it available for all concerns addressed. As a design aspect, this constitutes a major challenge for the success of a Global Marshall Plan.

Starting from an initiative step on the part of the EU Parliament und the EU Commission in autumn 2004, and with the date for **Rio+15** in mind, the campaign's timetable envisions a process leading towards a decision in 2007 for an implementation program starting in 2008. In this way, the extensive considerations of the World Summit in Rio 1992 would be realized to a considerable degree.

The **design process for a Global Marshall Plan** is a big challenge in itself. This is especially true for the **new forms of implementation** in international development cooperation, which are imperative and a **prerequisite for the success of the Initiative**. In the future, reflections to this end should be coordinated reciprocally between (1) governments and international organizations, (2) the internationally operating corporations, and (3) non-governmental organizations, in support of an advisory board to be convened by the European Union.

This report to the Global Marshall Plan Initiative / Planetary Contract presents an input to such a process. Furthermore, the **United Nations**, the **World Business Council on Sustainable Development** and the **Club of Rome** could assume an important coordinating role for the fields of action mentioned.

The text at hand is a continuation of the respective result document [90] of the EU project Terra 2000. It concludes a series of contributions made by the author and various research partners in the context of the EU-sponsored Project TERRA (www.terra-2000.org); please refer to, e.g. [69, 78, 79, 90].

I. Global Marshall Plan Initiative: Conceptional Background

During the last decades, many international leaders and thinkers have developed a program capable of steering global processes into a new, better direction. As is often the case, however, it proves highly difficult to proceed from extensive considerations to concrete measures, particularly where substantial economic transfers are involved. It is crucial to create an understanding that, in the current situation of worldwide problems, international development efforts to eradicate poverty are to everybody's advantage. An Eco-Social Market Economy provides an adequate framework for improving the situation, linking the equalization of standards to adequate co-financing measures in order to reach a **win-win Situation** for all stakeholders. An Eco-Social Planetary Contract provides an instrument for accomplishing a substantial intermediate step towards a **future reconcilable with sustainability** until 2015, and has the potential to induce a **global economic miracle**.

The Global Marshall Plan Initiative (www.globalmarshallplan.org) was initiated on May 16, 2003 by deputies of sixteen non-governmental organizations (ranging from environmental organizations, charitable trusts, development agencies, church representatives, deputies from industrial organizations, the Club of Rome and the Club of Budapest, to members of Attac) during a convention of the initiative for world peace, sustainability and equity (www.initiative-weltfrieden.org). The Global Contract Foundation assumes a coordinating function (project leader: **Surjo R. Soekadar**), the Club of Budapest initiated a larger publicity campaign, the Eco-Social Forum Europe promotes the topic Europe-wide and the University of Stuttgart and the Breuninger Foundation have funded a corresponding fellowship professor position of **Prof. Ervin Lazlo**, president of the Club of Budapest. Furthermore, the entrepreneurs **Karolin and Frithjof Finkbeiner** have established an independent foundation, the **"Global Marshall Plan Foundation"**, for the funding of accompanying measures. It aims at an initiating effect and invites other thinkers, doers and benefactors who wish to address this topic. As early as 2003, the **Federal Association for Business**

Promotion and Foreign Trade (BWA) has joined the Initiative as the first industrial organization, and so did the board of directors of **"Universitäts.Club Klagenfurt"** (www.uniclub.uni-klu.ac.at). The latter had publicly stepped forward with an interesting **"Friuli Manifesto"** [130].

Please refer to the website (www.globalmarshallplan.org) and the appendix of this text for further information on the Initiative's state of affairs, on the persons and the organizers involved, on the workshops as well as the **Declaration of Stuttgart** and its circle of signatories. Please also refer to the **Initiative's current positioning paper on the subject-matter** [70], scheduled to be published as paperback in 2004, and a related early statement by this author, added to the appendix of this text.

As mentioned, the long-term objective of the Initiative for a Global Marshall Plan is the worldwide implementation of an **Eco-Social Market Economy** [87, 93], a system of **high potential for value-adding** and **worldwide solidarity**, a so-called **Balanced Way**. It has been inspired substantially by the document "Crossing the Divide. Dialogue among Civilizations" initiated by **Kofi Annan** [3], by **Mikhail Gorbachev's** "My Manifesto for the Earth" [34], **Al Gore's** "Earth in the Balance - Ecology and the Human Spirit" [35], **Hans Küng's** "World Ethos" [62], the text on human responsibilities published by **Helmut Schmidt** [100], and finally, by the **Earth Charter** [117]. A dedicated **Initiative for an Ecological Marshall Plan** should not go unmentioned; it was initiated in 1997 by mentors like **Franz Alt, Carlhanns Damm, Wolfgang Engelhardt, Joschka Fischer, Maximilian Gege, Jo Leinen, Eva Quistorp, Wolfgang Rauls and Lutz Wicke** and succeeded in collecting approximately 750,000 signatures for the proposed plans [2]. Other important references, e.g. to **Susan Sontag** and **Lothar Späth**, can be found under [21, 28, 31, 32, 32, 37, 44, 63, 64, 65, 77, 84, 87, 97, 98, 99, 101, 107, 110]. A special mention should be made of the **World Future Council** currently being established by **Jakob von Uexküll** and **Maximilian Gege** [132], with whom we cooperate. The World Future Council's General Secretariat is located in Hamburg; this initiative's German coordinator is B.A.U.M., the largest environmental industry organization in Europe with approximately 500 participating companies.

As regards content, there is a connection to the **new house for experiencing knowledge**, the **ODYSSEUM Cologne and the Odysseum World Network**, which is currently being developed with an important coordinating role assumed by the author [74, 75].

Al Gore

"... if we cannot embrace the preservation of the Earth as our new organizing principle, the very survival of our civilization will be in doubt."

An Eco-Social Market Economy takes up **Carl Friedrich von Weizsäcker's** notion of the necessity for a **Global Domestic Policy** [7, 81, 133] while simultaneously emphasizing the value-adding potential of markets on innovation and growth. However, this potential must be imbedded in an adequate regulatory framework for economies, focusing not solely on the economical but also on the **social, cultural and ecological aspects** of human livelihoods. This embraces a modified view on man by economic sciences. Studies in **empirical economics** clearly proved such an idea of man to be much closer to reality than the abstract classical construction of a **homo oeconomicus** (e.g. in the context of the so-called **Ultimatum Bargain Game** [16, 78]).

The homo oeconomicus stands for the notion "If everybody cares for him/herself, everybody is cared for". It was this philosophy which led us into the problematic situation we face today, namely by providing one of the justification elements of market fundamentalism and turbo capitalism. Intriguingly, market fundamentalists like to refer to **Adam**

Smith as founder and chief witness for their idea of a free market, despite the fact that the original texts by this important thinker reveal much more differentiated reflections regarding the nature of economic processes. In particular, Adam Smith has always and persuasively maintained that governmental regimes are needed as regulating framework for markets; and in doing so has expressed highly differentiated views on **basic ethical and moral principles** [95, 116].

The perception of man as **homo oeconomicus cooperativus** seems much more realistic than the market-fundamentalist view [46]. Indeed, it seems safe to say that people are acting systematically non-systematic. This new scientific view on the nature of human beings has been impressively acknowledged by awarding Daniel Kahneman and Vernon L. Smith the Nobel Prize for economics in 2002.

Besides adopting a new idea of man, it is equally imperative that **prices tell the truth**, i.e. that **external costs are adequately internalized into market development**, amongst other things. This applies especially to international mobility, which today is too cheap when compared to the direct and indirect damages it induces (alongside many positive effects) and which indirectly leads to enormous market distortions, particularly for goods of low added value. Furthermore, competition needs to be promoted in order to avoid (de facto) monopolies, and support small and medium sized companies. The quintessential principle is that economy is meant for man, not man for economy; that for achieving effective wealth, growth, and progress for everyone, a strong and efficient state is required, and for a globalized economy, strong and efficient **structures of Global Governance (primacy of politics)** [27, 31, 32, 40, 41, 44, 63, 64, 69, 78, 79, 81, 87, 93, 106, 113, 117, 141, 142].

The concrete measures to be taken at this stage are: to overcome blockades towards the **advancement of the WTO**, and to link the WTO to other global regimes dealing with **security, economy, finance, environment, social issues, cultural balance and governance**, thus aiming for a **consistent global regime and institutional framework**. That such a consistent regulatory framework is missing may be the biggest flaw in the current global situation, because it entails that in many cases, what is collectively aspired by societies worldwide is diametrically opposed to what is profitable on markets. This is one of the reasons why the international community is making no progress in, e.g., **eradicating hunger** despite perpetual ample declarations and resolutions [25, 106].

Kofi Annan
[4, S. 61]

"True peace also means economic development and social justice, means protection of the global environment and damming of world-wide drug trafficking, means democracy, variety and dignity, respect of human rights and rule of law and much more."

The highly recommendable 2004 **ILO Report** on the **social aspects of globalization** [47], under the responsibility of the ILO World Commission on this topic, comes to the same conclusion. In newsletter 1/2004 of the Global Contract Foundation, Nicolai Sune Andersen gives the following summary of this report [6]:

ILO report on the social dimension of globalization

Summary by Nicolai Sune Andersen

"At the end of February, the Independent Global Committee convened by the ILO submitted a report on the social dimension of globalization. Our curator, Prof. Dr. Ernst Ulrich von Weizsäcker, was a member of this committee. The central assumptions and structural demands of the committee are presented here.

The report voices the fact that the public debate on globalization is about to derail. Communication is conditioned by deadlocked positions fragmented into a multiplicity of private interests. And the volition to reach a consensus is smallish. Currently, major international negotia-

tions are deadlocked, and international commitments to spur development are not met by and large.

The Committee was established by the ILO two years ago, and was headed by the president of Tanzania, Benjamin William Mkapa, and the Finnish president Tarja Halonen. The Committee members besides Prof. Dr. Ernst Ulrich von Weizsäcker included personages as diverse as, e.g., Joseph Stiglitz, Nobel Prize winner and former chief economist of the World Bank, Eveline Herfkens, chief coordinator of the UN campaign for the Millennium Development Goals and former minister of development of the Netherlands, and as representative of private enterprise, Taizo Nishimuro, chairman of Toshiba."

The report analyses the earth's current economic situation. Amongst others, the following theses are set up:

- *Since 1980, the growth of world gross domestic product (GDP) has decreased in comparison to the preceding decades. The committee maintains that this fact "disputes the optimistic prognoses on the effects globalization has on growth".*

- *The distribution of growth per capita is very unequal, both among the developed countries and among the developing countries. Between 1985 and 2000, the growth of merely 16 developing countries exceeded 3 percent, while it was less than 2 percent in 55 countries, including 23 with negative growth.*

- *The income gap between the richest and the poorest countries has widened enormously. The difference in average incomes has mounted from US$ 212 versus US$ 11, 417 between 1960 and 1962, to US$ 267 versus US$ 32, 339 between 2000 and 2002.*

- *The economic development in developing countries increasingly dropped behind that of industrialized countries between 1991 and 2001, resulting in a state of the world where 22 industrialized countries with only about 14 % of the world population dominate half of world trade and more than half of worldwide foreign direct investments (FDI).*

- *On a global level, unemployment has further increased in 2003. The number of unemployed people seeking jobs has transgressed the number of 185 million, amounting to 6.2 percent of the total work force; this is the highest unemployment rate ever registered by the ILO. Particularly affected are approximately 82 million young people aged between 15 and 24, most of them living in developing countries, with an unemployment rate of 14.4 percent.*

- *The "informal economy" comprised predominantly of people without steady employment or income will further extend, particularly in countries with low GDP growth. The situation is aggravated by the growing number of people hunting the decreasing number of jobs. At the same time, the number of the "working poor" - individuals living on US$ 1 a day or less - has stabilized in 2003. Their numbers amount to an estimated 550 million people worldwide.*

- *The growth of foreign direct investments (FDI) increased at the beginning of the Eighties. In 2000, more than 100 countries had introduced major liberalization measures in favor of increased FDI. However, "many expectations have not been satisfied "according to the committee. Despite the high growth rates in foreign direct investments (FDI) in developing countries, most of the investments have been concentrated in 10 of these countries.*

- *Development assistance on the whole has been reduced, and is well below the declared goal of 0.7 percent of GDP, with a current average of 0.23 percent. If the goal of 0.7 % had been reached, development assistance would have increased by an additional sum of US$ 100 billion per year. The report states that "we should give our vote to those who demand that the goals are respected. If in the last 30 years all countries had met the targets, we would have US$ 2.5 trillion more to spend on development."*

- *The implementation of the Millennium Development Goals (MDG) is jeopardized. At least US$ 50 billion annually are required additionally to achieve these goals until 2015. Even if the donor countries meet their promise made at the summit in Monterrey to increase development assistance by US$ 16 billion until 2006, we are still short of two thirds of the minimal funds required to reach the goals Against this background, the committee demands that the social dimension of the globalization debate is enforced. The current developments promote a state of imbalance both within and between the countries. The report invites engagement for development activities with a strong social dimension, based on common universal values, respect for the human rights and democratic forms of government, which carry possibilities and gains for all countries and people. The following points should receive special attention:*

  - *Focus on people*
  - *A democratic and effective state*
  - *Sustainable development*
  - *Productive and equitable markets*
  - *Globalization with solidarity*
  - *More responsibility towards the peoples*
  - *Stronger, more comprehensive partnership*
  - *An effective UN system*

The committee recommends a set of reforms on a global level, e.g. concerning international trade and the PRSP process (Poverty Reduction Strategy Paper) under the direction of World Bank and IMF. Furthermore, the committee suggests that developing countries are granted more influence within the international financial institutions.

The developing countries' representation within the decision-making bodies of the Bretton Woods Institutions should be enforced. Additionally, the working methods of the World Trade Organization (WTO) should be adapted to guarantee an effective participation of these countries in negotiations. As regards international trade, the committee demands amongst other things that "global rules pertaining to trade and financial policy should provide more space for autonomous policies in developing countries". Concerning the PRSP process, the committee stresses the point that this process "should no longer generate those structural adaptation programs which failed to work because of the dogmatic demands for privatization and reduced public services". The committee concludes that the process needs to be closely supervised.

Because of the importance of these elaborations, we continue by citing the first 12 positions of the study [47] (accentuations added by the author of this text). The document is very worth reading and contains many findings that are expressed similarly in the text at hand.

- *The current path of globalization must change. Too few share in its benefits. Too many have no voice in its design and no influence on its course.*

- *The results of globalization are what we make of it. They depend on the policies, rules and institutions which governs its course; the values which inspire its actors; and their capacity to influence the process.*

- *We, the members of the* **World Commission** *represent a very wide diversity of opinion and interests, which are often polarized in the public debates on globalization. But we have come to agreement on a common goal;* ***a fair globalization which creates opportunities for all.*** *We wish to make globalization a means to expand human well-being and freedom, and to bring democracy and development to local communities where people live. Our aim is to build a consensus for common action to realize this vision, and to foster a process of sustained engagement to this end by the actors themselves, including States, international organizations, business, labour, and civil society.*

- *Ours is a critical but positive message. We believe the benefits of globalization can be expanded; its results better shared; and many of its problems resolved. The resources and the means are at hand. Our proposals are ambitious but feasible. We are certain that* ***a better world is possible****.*

- *We seek a process which is fair, and which gives all women and men the rights, opportunities and capabilities they need to exercise their own choices for a decent life.*

- *We reaffirm the* ***value of values****, and the importance of human rights in guiding the governance of globalization, and in defining the responsibilities of its actors.*

- *We call for a more cohesive governance of globalization with policies to better link economic growth with social progress and environmental sustainability.*

- *We must be realistic. Globalization has many aspects, but our mandate is to focus on its social dimension. We also recognize the many different dialogues and initiatives which are under way and seek to encourage and build on them.*

- ***Globalization is being judged by what it delivers**. Although many of the ills of the world today - poverty, the lack of decent work, the denial of human rights existed long before the present phase of globalization, there has been growing exclusions and deprivation in certain regions of the world. For many, **globalization has dislocated traditional livelihoods and local communities**, and threatens environmental sustainability and cultural diversity. As the current process of crossborder interaction and interconnectivity gathers speed, there is increasing debate not only about inequalities between countries but also about inequalities within countries, and its effects on people, families and communities. These concerns lie at the heart of politics. **The debate on globalization is fast becoming a debate on democracy and social justice in a global economy**.*

- *We recognize that globalization has opened the door to many benefits. It has promoted **open societies** and open economies and encouraged a freer exchange of goods, ideas and knowledge. In many parts of the world, innovation, creativity, and entrepreneurship have flourished. In East Asia, growth lifted over 200 million people out of poverty in a single decade. Better communications have enhanced awareness of rights and identities, and enabled social movements to mobilize opinion and strengthen democratic accountability. As a result, a **truly global conscience is beginning to emerge**, sensitive to the inequities of poverty, gender discrimination, child labour, and environmental degradation, wherever these may occur.*

- *Yet there is growing concern about the direction globalization is currently taking. Its advantages are too distant for too many, while its risks are all too real. Its volatility threatens both rich and poor. Immense riches are being generated. But fundamental problems of poverty, exclusion and inequality persist. Corruption is widespread. Open societies are threatened by global terrorism, and the future of open markets is increasingly in question. Global Governance is in crisis. We are at a critical juncture, and we need to urgently rethink our current policies and institutions.*

Where do we stand today?

- *There are deep-seated and persistent imbalances in the current workings of the global economy, which are* ***ethically unacceptable*** *and* ***politically unsustainable****. They arise from a fundamental imbalance between the economy, society, and the polity. The economy is becoming increasingly global, while social and political institutions remain largely local, national or regional. None of the existing global institutions provide adequate democratic oversight of global markets, or redress basic inequalities between countries.* ***These imbalances point to the need for better institutional frameworks and policies*** *if the promise of globalization is to be realized.*

The report by the ILO World Commission provides many important indications, e.g. concerning the insufficient implementation of the UN Millennium Development Goals. Yet the proposals made are rather cautious, which is true for all discerning international reports. The "Think big" approach is not a very realistic one on the international stage, as all past experience shows. Still, it steers into the right direction. The approach taken by a Global Marshall Plan / Planetary Contract includes all this, but tries to take a **big step** beyond it, pledging to finally transform plans and hopes into solutions and implementation successes. This reflects a point of view inspired by **game theoretical considerations**, claiming that today's highly complex issues cannot be met by small steps in individual areas, but call for a larger concept covering multiple topics, because only such a step can provide **"enough adjusting knobs"** for multifaceted win-win constellations which benefit all.

In this, the supporters of the Initiative are not isolated. Rather, the development of a new consensus can finally be observed, which may be capable of **replacing the market-fundamentalist Washington Consensus** of the Nineties that has already caused widespread devastation on this globe. This new consensus can reassert the importance of a general economical framework and the state's role in ensuring wealth and welfare in terms of an **Ordoliberalism** [9, 44, 47, 88, 89, 109, 115, 130, 131, 135, 146]. The version of the **Washington Consensus** as printed in [56], authored by the economist John Williamson (1989), lists the following 10 propositions:

- Fiscal discipline
- A redirection of public expenditure priorities toward fields offering both high economic returns and the potential to improve income distribution
- Tax reform (to lower marginal rates and broaden the tax-base)
- Liberalization of the capital market
- A stable, competitive exchange rate
- Trade liberalization
- Abolition of market access barriers / Liberalization of inflows of foreign direct investment (equal treatment of foreign and domestic firms)
- Privatization
- Deregulation (to abolish barriers to entry and exit)
- Secure property rights

These arguments sound good, like so many presented by market fundamentalists. It is however quite obvious that if part of this is implemented in the current form and under the factual conditions of today's world politics, achieving the social objectives expressed here will be virtually impossible. A policy following this logic requires, e.g., that to receive credit from the International Monetary Fund, poor countries have to cutback on their government expenditures, further degrading these countries' education and health systems at the expense of the already deprived population. How is development ever to be achieved if the vital determinants of sustainability, education and health are systematically degraded? **Thus, this consensus must urgently be replaced by something better**. This is a special concern of **Guido Eberhard** [22].

For the successful establishment of a consistent regime in the context of a Global Marshall Plan, through co-financing measures and under inclusion of the WTO, all future loans from IMF and World Bank should take the central elements of ILO, UNESCO, and UNEP standards into consideration. Incidentally, such interventions are currently dismissed as interfering with the sovereignty of the receiving countries, ignoring the massive intervention imposed by the loan conditions regarding e.g. the size of the country's public sector. While in the context of the Washington Consensus these are selective interventions at the expense of social balance and sustainability, interventions in the future context of a Global Marshall Plan will hopefully be in support of sustainability.

The concrete objective of an consistent ordoliberal regime is the establishment of appropriate worldwide standards which comply with sustainability concerns. For understandable reasons, finding an agreement with the developing countries on high standards will generally depend on **co-financing measures** and **coordinated further market openings** by developed countries for the benefit of the rest of the world, most notably the poorest states. Again, this should be based on adequate conditions, agreed upon in fair negotiations - as requested by the developing countries at all related summits during the last decades. Co-financing measures in combination with the establishment of standards - possibly dependent on a country's state of development - is also the central **design element and crucial concern of an Eco-Social Market Economy** [83, 97].

Examples for the successful implementation of the basic principle "co-financing in return for adjustment of standards" are the successful **Protocol of Montreal** for the protection of the earth's ozone layer or, e.g., the **Marshall Plan of the US** for the reconstruction of Europe after World War II, which followed a similar logic and relied substantially on the **opening of the US market for the receiving countries**. To an even stronger degree, the **EU enlargement processes** [87] provide a positive example for the eco-social approach. A lot can be learned for the future development of the world from the EU approach, which connects the adjustment of standards to the opening of markets and co-financing measures, ultimately leading to **open borders** and an **open society.**

Javier Solana *European Council*

"As a union of 25 states with over 450 million people producing a quarter of the world's gross national product (GDP), the European Union is a global actor; it should be ready to share in the responsibility for global security."

While co-financing and opening of markets are crucial points, they require **complementary efforts on the national level**. However, co-financing measures are not readily rendered and **counter-arguments are easily found**. For this reason, debates on co-financing tend to be conducted in a way as if stressing the necessity of global solidarity would detract from the importance of an adequate national implementation. The entailing danger of waning local efforts because of foreign support measures can be dismissed as a minor danger as long as the international transfers continue to be relatively small, and the issues continue to be extreme and serious. More often than not, the ones who invariably and exclusively refer to domestic challenges yet to be met by the poorer countries seem to be most concerned about being spared the cost themselves.

Referring to **Europe as an example** point of reference for worldwide solutions shall not insinuate that, from a global perspective, the European model was perfect. The same applies when tying in with a US activity for Europe by quoting the Marshall Plan. There is no denying the prevalently critical global assessment of any of the US aid programs. Nor that the current rate of resource exhaustion and environmental pollution in Europe, not to mention the US, are unacceptable in the long run. It must however be noted in this context that there are limits as to how far one part of the world, e.g. Europe, can lead the way, when others operate differently and are rewarded for it in an **ill-ordered world of free trade** (prisoner's dilemma situation [87]).

There can also be no doubt that owing to its **colonial past**, Europe is not ubiquitously regarded kindly in this world, and that most countries would reject the idea of adopting a model inspired by Europe. In the current tense state of world politics, the term 'Marshall" in relation to the US already constitutes a problem for many who have never heard of the beneficial effects of the Marshall Plan. Therefore, the term **"Eco-Social Global Marshall Plan"** is used primarily within Europe and interactions with dialogue partners in the US. In other contexts, it is better described in terms like **Eco-Social Market Economy**, **Planetary Contract**, **World Solidarity Plan**, or **Balanced Way**. In order to maintain a better balance in this respect, the Initiative uses the title **Global Marshall Plan / Planetary Contract**, with the second half of the name carrying at least as much importance as the first. In conclusion, we wish to stress the point that the naming of the plan does not insinuate a **naive overvaluation of Europe or the West**, or the developed world, respectively. Quite the contrary, at least as much knowledge as can be contributed by the West has to be incorporated from other parts of the world. Against this background, the **positive appreciation of European political approaches**, as well as the **idea of the Marshall Plan**,is focused on the following points, which are constitutive of the approach taken:

1.) The willingness to play a part in **international contracts** while favoring consensus (e.g. the UN Convention on the Rights of the Child, the Kyoto Protocol, the International Criminal Court).

2.) A strong commitment to **environmental protection**. That is, to the extent that no disadvantages result on the world market.

3.) Substantial investment in a **high social balance** within and among the European countries.

4.) Substantial investment in promoting **cultural diversity and tolerance** within Europe.

5.) The willingness to open markets and take **substantial co-financing measures** for the EU enlargement processes, plus at the very least the intention to **further open markets internationally and co-finance development matters** in the context of a common observance of standards; this again under the stipulation that its own competitiveness is not impaired. It should not go unnoticed that Europe, despite the need to do more, today accounts for 70 % of worldwide development assistance (www.global-society-dialogue.org).

This implies that on the whole, Europe (still) favors the "mega philosophy" [58] of an **Eco-Social Market Economy over**

market fundamentalism, provided that the objective of maintaining competitiveness under adverse global circumstances does not enforce a different position. Unfortunately, the latter is sometimes the case nowadays, and one of the causes of irritations currently affecting the political debate in Europe [88].

In this context, there is **no neo-colonial arrogance** in following experience of the EU enlargement processes. Rather, we use some successful principles of European economical philosophy (i.e., market means competition subject to adequate regulatory principles) as basis for a global strategy. This strategy **builds on a broad background of international considerations** that the author has been involved in for more than ten years as a member of many policy advisory boards [27, 48, 69, 78, 79, 84, 85, 99, 117].

The basic position acquired in this process is not specifically European, but was compiled with the collaboration of representatives from all regions of the world in the context of a **Global Society Dialogue** (www.global-society-dialogue.org [33]) initiated by the EU. The respective reflections have at the same time been substantially inspired by the world ethos process [61, 63, 64, 65], which includes all major religions of the world, as well as the complementary **Earth Charter** Process [117] based on humanist tradition, and have found significant support from global networks of planetary-oriented thinkers like the **Club of Rome** and the **Club of Budapest**.

Since the days of **Mahatma Gandhi**, the principle of "co-financing of development under the condition of alignment of standards" is a central position expressed at all international conferences, in particular by the poorer or developing countries. Most recently, this surfaced again during the preliminary negotiations for the **World Summit on the Information Society**. In Geneva, a blockade similar to the last WTO meeting in Cancun was imminent. It evolved around a central request made by the developing countries concerning a special budget, a so-called **"Digital Solidarity Fund"**, designed to contribute to overcoming the digital divide between the North and the South. As always at this point, the rich countries stalled [57]. The same pattern could be observed at the meeting of the **Organization of American States** (OAS) in Montevideo (Uruguay) in January 2004. While the US were intent on discussing free trade, liberalization and the fight against terrorism, most of the Central- and South American states centered on the **eradication of poverty**. However, the demanded **poverty fund** did not find approval and was dismissed by the US in particular. According to US president George W. Bush, programs like this exist in abundance already. **It's obviously as simple as that.**

Mahatma Gandhi

"The earth has enough for everyone's needs but not for everyone's greed."

While co-financing of development is **indispensable and well-founded**, accordant contracts must be supplemented by corresponding duties on the part of the receiving countries, and must be agreed upon at eye-to-eye level, as has always been the case in EU enlargement processes. Respective mechanisms have long been **applied within all effectively operating states**, essentially ensuring balance, coherence, and welfare.

In the author's view, **one to two percent of the (world) gross national product** must be put forth as the volume of co-financing measures taken for the cooperation intended [87]. Other experts, with the scale of the **EU structure funds** as one of the best instruments of EU policy in mind, believe that a lower volume of 0.3 to 0.5 % will be sufficient if correctly deployed [53]. The funds can be raised through various mechanisms, e.g. direct payments by states according to their gross national product, as applied in the EU, or through the **taxation of internationally utilized resources or pro-**

cesses which are critical ecologically, directly related to globalization, or **which gain from globalization**.

As an alternative to the latter, funds could be raised from **fair trade** with rights for resource utilization or pollution. This could be achieved with an intelligent development of the Kyoto Protocol for the time after 2012 [87], e.g. in form of a **market and incentive-oriented global climate certificate system** [136, 137]. In this context, sums of **two- to three-digit billion dollar per year** could be mobilized in the future (ref. chapter V); and the North would be paying for something that belongs to others from a fair, ethical point of view, but which it has been consuming massively and at no charge up to now. Moreover, the **International Finance Facility** (IFF) proposed by British Chancellor of the Exchequer **Gordon Brown** is highly interesting, which is described in detail elsewhere in this text (compare [12, 13, 47]).

For reasons of simplicity and political feasibility, the author considers a **transfer of Special Drawing Rights of the IMF** to the developing countries, a **Tobin tax on international financial transactions** and **taxes on worldwide trade** (in particular telecommunication, energy consumption, agricultural economy, pharmaceutical products, military expenses) to be especially eligible. A **tax in the context of brain-drain** or, as mentioned, a sensible international regime for **trading emission rights for carbon dioxide** (equally distributed per capita) in continuation of the Kyoto Protocol, would be appropriate measures but unlikely to be practicable until 2015, neither politically nor in terms of implementation, according to this document's logic [77, 87, 136, 137]. This latter issue must be tackled in the coming negotiations on the Climate Convention.

Equally important as raising more funds is to use these funds solely for their designated purpose, and linked to the **implementation of certain standards**, e.g. pertaining to environmental and social issues (ref. chapter II). They must not flow predominantly or substantially into the pockets of local elites for consumerism.

A worldwide Eco-Social Market Economy is regarded as the natural framework for achieving an **open society** [108, 109]; this is especially true against the background of the current transition into a **worldwide information and knowledge society**, in itself bearing special chances, but also risks [27, 30, 33, 48, 57, 69, 78, 79, 81, 84, 85, 117]. These risks are predominantly associated with so-called **rebound effects** of technological progress, resulting from an inadequate regulatory framework for the economy [73, 87, 130].

As has been illustrated, an Eco-Social Market Economy relies on the power of markets and competition, but it has to be subject to an eco-social regulatory framework at the same time. Thus, its objective is growth under the terms of appropriate **de-materialization conditions** (**factor 4 / factor 10 concepts, closed loop recycling management, Eco-efficiency and Eco-effectiveness**), (ref. [10, 11, 87, 102, 134]). **Eco-effectiveness** calls for doing the right things, in which the term distinguishes itself from the concept of efficiency which is solely concerned with cause-effect relations. Linking both approaches, i.e. the **efficient implementation of effective strategies**, obviously has a particularly high potential.

The eco-social approach seems to be the vastly superior model compared to an increasingly deregulated world economy under the terms of the **market-fundamentalist** mega-philosophy dominant today. In terms of material results, the latter creates a **bottom-to-top** redistribution on an unacceptably high level both nationally and internationally [78], and leaves individual countries as well as the whole world **poorer than it could be** under eco-social conditions.

The objective is therefore a **better design of globalization**, which is indeed possible! This is a central request of the people behind the Initiative for a Global Marshall Plan, the ILO World Commission on the Social Dimension of Globalization cited above [47], of many observers interested in world politics, and particularly of the global movement **ATTAC** [38], which explicitly pursues the cause of a **better design of globalization** [31, 32]. The world could be more balanced, peaceful and, above all, more wealthy than it is today. However, this requires a change in worldwide distribution patterns; in particular **investment in fully unfolding all human potential** on this globe, providing all human beings with **infrastructure at a sufficient scale**, and ensuring **access to required resources** for all. All this can only be achieved under reasonable (world) societal regimes that must be enforced internationally, no different from what has been achieved in historical processes in all states which are successful today. Succeeding with this carries the chance for a desperately needed **global economic miracle** [78, 90].

"Public investments in poor people spur economic growth, while economic growth sustains such investments."

from: Millennium Development Compact [126]

Intermediate steps are needed on the road to a worldwide Eco-Social Market Economy. That our situation requires a fundamentally new approach has become particularly apparent in the face of the **failure of the most recent WTO development round in Cancun** in the fall of 2003, but also the obvious problems the US face in Iraq, the recent **"offences of fraud"** on national and international finance markets, and the **"looting"** of global ecological resources and sinks, e.g. where climate is concerned.

Additionally, we need to understand the force of the **processes' own momentum**, the special rhythms of national development, and the **large timeframes** required for the worldwide transformation processes in the form necessary today [1].

This refers, among others, to the balancing of tensions implied in terms like regulation vs. self-responsibility, industrialization vs. environment, valuing global public goods vs. market scepticism, Old vs. New, dialogue vs. impact, need for global problem-solving vs. current power imbalances, national identity vs. transnational governance, promises vs. implementation [68]. A sense of **feasibility of change**, as well as **patience** is of the highest importance in this context.

Václav Havel

"One cannot merely follow the timetable we have set for our influence on the world, we must also honour and respect the infinitely more complex timetable the world has set for itself. That timetable is the sum of the thousands of independent timetables of an infinite number of natural, historical and human actions."

It was **Albert Einstein** who observed that problems could not be solved by applying the same logic which has caused them. **Friedrich Hölderlin** gives us hope that where problems grow, solutions do, too. A Global Marshall Plan as an example for a Planetary Contract includes both: **a new logic** and, hopefully, the potential for **solving** many of the current problems worldwide.

The seven deadly sins of the world

Wealth without work
Pleasure without conscience
Knowledge without character
Commerce without morality
Science without humanity
Worship without sacrifice
Politics without principle

Mahatma Ghandi

II. Pressure to Act, Innovative Solutions, Coherent Institutional Design, New Mechanisms of Implementation

The economic "cost" of worldwide poverty (i.e., to forsake prosperity potentials) and its political "risks" (i.e., destructive conflicts, terrorism) are no longer acceptable. This also applies to the "rich" on this planet, whose wealth and security is threatened by such conditions, while chances for increasing prosperity are diminished. If we wish to ensure a prosperous future, there is no realistic peaceful alternative to supporting the development of markets in the "South". Most importantly, private enterprise is called upon to design this **global "win-win game"** in a constructive way.

Considerations on a Global Marshall Plan / Planetary Contract are propelled by the intolerable nature of the current global situation, a fact that is becoming more and more evident to all observers. If global environmental problems are not tackled head on, if prosperity remains a property of the rich only, and if the incredibly huge divide between rich and poor remains, devastating crises and catastrophes will be imminent, especially in the form of **clashes between cultures**. We approach states that can no longer be insured and which threaten the future economic development substantially. The signs of hopelessness and aggression become increasingly hard to ignore [87, 90, 93] both globally and locally. The latter is largely caused by the forced reconversion of the social systems in Europe in the wake of the current globalization processes which leaves 80 percent of the population poorer than before, albeit incurring substantial profits for a small group [78, 87, 88].

This trend follows the direction of current global distribution patterns. It can only be stopped if we manage to shift globalization into a new direction. This even became a point of discussion at the last annual meeting of the World Trade Forum in Davos [9]. Similar thoughts have been expressed by **Horst Köhler**, until recently Executive Director of the International Monetary Fund [59] and now elected President of Germany.

In the author's view, there are but two possibilities left in the wake of globalization and the effects of the current world structure: Either the world structure stays the same; then the social balance in Europe will be lost forever (the current reconversion process then being only the beginning), or the world structure on the whole is steered towards the implementation of social concerns; then the social balance can be permanently sustained in Europe and in the highly developed Asian countries, though under the presumption that the US, too, shifts back into this direction.

Anyone concerned with the social balance in Europe or the particular interests of at least 80 percent of the European population will sensibly invest in a worldwide social balance and therefore, as a first step, in a Global Marshall Plan / Planetary Contract. With regard to the worldwide threat of **social devastations**, possibly cumulating in more and more terrorism, as well as to looming environmental catastrophes, this is in the best interest of the richest 20 percent of the population in the developed countries, including the US. Terms like "**insightful**" or "**enlightened selfishness**" may thus add an additional motivation in favor of the approach taken here, besides ethical considerations.

Co-financing standards worldwide requires linkage to adequate regional measures, for example within the EU. From the Club of Rome and the Arab Thought Forum stems the ambitious proposal of an over-regional management of **energy and water reserves**, in perfect compliance with the considerations presented here. The same applies to a corresponding proposition for co-operation in the energy sector between Europe and the countries of the Southern Mediterranean, especially where the application of **renewable ener-**

gies [121] is concerned. The latter are of major importance, both in view of **worldwide shortages in the energy sector** imminent from 2015 onwards [69], and the **US Energy Strategy for 2020** [92], which is alarmingly geared towards further increases in consumption. In the light of climate concerns and a recent **Pentagon Study** [103] on oil, this strategy becomes even more irritating.

Reasonable worldwide co-financing of development, in connection with further opening of markets by rich countries in a sustainable manner, and implemented in close reciprocity to the establishment of standards, has the potential of inducing a **global economic miracle** within the framework of a development adjusted to benefit all. To this end, regulatory processes need to be adequately linked to competitive mechanisms, connecting **human potentials, resources** and **infrastructures** with **well-considered institutional designs** to establish efficient value-adding systems.

A Coherent Global Governance System

The central design element of the proposal for a Global Marshall Plan / Planetary Contract is to take a decisive step towards a coherent global governance structure by **linking existing global regimes** in connection with the target of implementing the **UN Millennium Development Goals** which will be discussed further in the next paragraph. Without this long overdue step, a positive worldwide development will hardly be possible. Such a development can only be accomplished through contracts between the North and the South, **internalization of the cost of global environmental impacts into world economy**, and adequate prize structures. These measures are essential for steering the technological progress towards **massive dematerialization**, thus leading our **ways of life** in a sustainable direction.

Moreover, only such a step seems capable of ensuring **better local government** in many parts of the world, which in turn is a prerequisite of economical and societal development.

To be eligible for financial funding through a Global Marshall Plan for development, countries must accept and implement the **core standards of the International Labor Organization** (ILO Standards), certain **UNESCO** agreements concerning cultural diversity, as well as the **Global Environmental Agreements** (GEA) which are coordinated by the **United Nations Environment Programme** (UNEP). Simultaneously, this entails the basic implementation of the so-called **economic, social and cultural human rights** (www.ilo.org/public/english/bureau/gender/newsite2002/ standard/).

In 1995, these have finally gained the same fundamental and international status as the political individual human rights [139]. Having acquired this status shortly after the founding of the UN, the implementation of the latter is much more advanced, albeit remaining problems. An explicit integration of this extra dimension of human rights into a Planetary Contract should be considered. Additionally, the issue of an **anti-monopolistic authority** and a **more stringent control of offshore banking centers** should be tackled in this context, building on the current international efforts in this field. **Money alone solves no problems** - but it can help doing so.

"The goal of UN Secretary General Kofi Annan to reduce absolute poverty by 50 per cent until the year 2015 can only be reached with a fundamental change of attitude on solidarity between the countries of the North and the South."

Klaus Töpfer
Executive-Director of the United Nations Environment Programme UNEP

Therefore, the core demand of this proposal is that the North, by offering co-financing and further opening of its markets, finally ensures that developing countries are able to factually implement the standards aspired internationally, without suffering **economic disadvantages**. More often than not, these standards have already been signed but are routinely bypassed in interaction with international consumers.

As long as it is a major competitive advantage for economically lagging countries to disregard standards, it is "**hypocritical**" and a "**misinterpretation of the principle of equality"**, as well as a form of "**preferential self-treatment**" on the part of the rich countries to demand adherence to standards without offering co-financing measures. Thus, without co-financing no consensual contract on adhering standards, and consequently **no internalization of cost** related to global environmental and resource problems can be achieved, resulting in a lack of pressure to enforce dematerialization, innovation and new ways of life complying with the goal of sustainable development.

Consequently, the Global Marshall Plan Initiative aims for the successful linkage of ILO, UNESCO and global environmental standards - plus other standards where appropriate (e.g., the World Bank's Safeguard Policies and the ISO standards as indicated by **Maartje van Putten** [80]) - with WTO, International Monetary Fund and World Bank, to form a **coherent system of Global Governance**. This institutional set-up must include an adequate **supreme judicial body**, which could be institutionalized by linking various existing international legislative bodies, in particular the one pertaining to the WTO. The organization of this supreme body will become a central design challenge, as Maartje van Putten points out [80].

Achieving these goals would finally satisfy the demand of the developed countries and many NGOs that the core social standards of the ILO, the cultural consensus as adressed by UNESCO, the global environmental agreements, and the economic, social and cultural human rights are met in the WTO, and above all, that their implementation in world economics finally becomes mandatory, enforced mainly by the **sanction mechanisms of WTO, IMF and WB**.

Intriguingly, during WTO negotiations, such demands have repeatedly been made by the US who have as yet failed to ratify more than two of eight core ILO standards, while fulfilling all of them according to experts. Thus, their ratification should present no problem to the US.

What are the core ILO standards about?

The following eight agreements were declared basic agreements ("core agreements") by the ILO's executive council; the underlying principles are considered fundamental human rights (www.ilo.org/public/english/bureau/gender/newsite 2002/standard/).

- Convention (No. 87): Freedom of Association and Protection of the Right to Organize Convention, 1948
  (Workers and employers, without distinction whatsoever, shall have the right to establish and, subject only to the rules of the organization concerned, to join organizations of their own choosing without previous authorization).

- Convention (No. 98): Right to Organize and Collective Bargaining Convention, 1949
  (Workers shall enjoy adequate protection against acts of anti-union discrimination in respect of their employment. Workers' and employers' organizations shall enjoy adequate protection against any acts of interference by each other or each other's agents or members in their establishment, functioning or administration).

- Convention (No. 29): Forced Labor Convention, 1930
  (Call to abolish forced or compulsory labor in all its forms; certain exceptions apply in the military sector, with priso-

ners and in cases of emergency such as wars, conflagrations or earthquakes).

- Convention (No. 111): Discrimination (Employment and Occupation) Convention, 1958
(Abolition of any distinction, exclusion or preference made on the basis of race, color, sex, religion, political opinion, national extraction or social origin, which has the effect of nullifying or impairing equality of opportunity or treatment in employment or occupation).

- Convention (No. 100): Equal Remuneration Convention, 1951
(Equal rates of remuneration without discrimination based on sex).

- Convention (No. 138): Minimum Age Convention, 1973
(Ensure the effective abolition of child labor; the minimum age for admission to employment shall not be less than the age of completion of compulsory schooling).

- Convention (No. 182): Worst Forms of Child Labor Convention, 1999
(Immediate and effective measures to secure the prohibition and elimination of the worst forms of child labor as a matter of urgency).

Concerning the abolishment of Child Labor, a core concern of the ILO, the following cues from [129] are helpful:

A study by the International Labor Organization (ILO) says the benefits of elimination child labor will be nearly seven times greater than the costs. An estimate is US$ 5.1 trillion in the developing and transitional economies, where most child laborers are found. The study, conducted by the ILO International Programme on the Elimination of Child Labor (IPEC), says child labor - which *involves one in every six children in the world - can be eliminated and replaced by universal education by the year 2020 at an estimated total cost of US$ 760 billion. ILO estimates that some 246 million children are currently involved in child labor worldwide. Of these, 179 million - or one in every eight children worldwide - are exposed to the worst forms of child labor, which endanger their physical, mental or moral wellbeing.*

In comparison to other social costs, the average annual cost of elimination of child labor would be far less than the cost of financing debt service or the military, the study says. For example, the average annual cost of US$ 95 billion would amount to about 20 % of current military spending in developing and transitional countries, or 9.5 percent of developing countries US$ 1 trillion debt service. The study argues that the costs are a "wise investment" as each extra year of schooling stemming from universal education to the age of 14 results in an additional 11 % of future earnings per year, yielding global benefits of just over US$ 5 trillion. On the cost side, the supply of education accounts for nearly two-thirds of the total costs.

Demographic problems and the Millennium Development Goals

The Global Marshall Plan Initiative aims for the implementation of the **UN Millennium Development Goals** until 2015 as an intermediary step towards a worldwide Eco-Social Market Economy. These goals will be discussed in detail in the next paragraph. Many observers including the author believe that the potential accomplishment of the Millennium Development Goals depends significantly on a **dedicated tackling of the issue of world population growth** [1, 18, 19, 51, 54, 69, 83]. The demographic development has always been of vital importance to mankind. It is indispensable that the current growth is reversed [54]. To be in control of one's number of descendents is **a human right,** as stated under the term of **Reproductive Health** by the United Nations. Major keywords are, among others, "Women Rights", "Child Spacing", and "Reproductive Rights." The efficient UN body **UNFPA** (www.unfpa.org) addresses this topic independently, and has vastly contributed to an increased worldwide awareness of these issues. The **International Planned Parenthood Federation** [51] works with over 150 family planning organizations in at least 180 countries worldwide to promote sexual and reproductive health, freedom of choice, and the rights of men, women and young people.

The **World Population Conference in Cairo 1994** - International Conference on Population and Development - was a crucial event in this context, with 179 states deciding on a groundbreaking plan of action. Until 2015, all human beings were to be granted **access to a broad choice of family planning** measures and accompanying health care. A lot has since been achieved, but not all, and the targets set then are now facing conservative, partly **religious-fundamentalist resistance**, especially in the **US**. Consequently, the funds required and promised in Cairo have not been raised. Until 2000, expenditures were supposed to increase to US$17 billion per year, to US$ 18.5 billion until 2005, and to US$ 21.7 billion until 2015 (ref. [18, 19]).

Two thirds were supposed to be raised by the developing countries themselves, one third by the industrialized nations. **However, the payment morality of the rich world once again leaves a lot to be desired**. In 2001, the industrialized countries raised a total US$ 2.5 billion - significantly less than half of the agreed sum. The developing countries allocated US $7.1 billion, 63 percent of what was promised for the year 2000. Therefore, it is important that the rich countries increase their contribution by US$ 3 to 4 billion within the next few years. This point will be stressed again when discussing the financing of the Global Marshall Plan.

Because of its vital importance, the demographic issue is internationally dealt with by dedicated persons and organizations, though still at an insufficient scale. From the context the author is personally familiar with [94], the international initiative of the **Rotarian Fellowship for Population and Development**, RFPD (www.rfpd.de; www.rifpd.org) should be mentioned, as well as the **German Foundation for World Population** (www.dsw-online.de/english/index.html) and the **Population Institute in Washington**, USA (www.population-institute.org). In recent times, members of parliament around the world engage in issues of population and development.

"National strategies for the Millennium Development Goals must include a commitment to women's rights to education, reproductive health services, property ownership, secure tenure, and labour force participation."

Millennium Development Compact [126]

The United Nations stress this correlation between population growth and the Millennium Development Goals explicitly and in great detail [123], as does the German Federal Ministry for Economic Cooperation and Development (Bundesministerium für wirtschaftliche Zusammenarbeit und Entwicklung) in a special publication on the topic "Sexual and Reproductive Health" [15].

Religious fundamentalists in many parts of the world, particularly in the US, have been **jeopardizing the consensus of Cairo** and international strategies for the **enforcement of reproductive rights of people in poorer countries** since several years, aiming to deprive people in the poor world of what is a matter of course in the rich countries, i.e. the right to control the number of children one wishes to have, and to be granted the necessary information and technical means. The US were the **only country** which explicitly dismissed the **human right for reproductive self-determination** during the annual conference of the UN Human Rights Commission in Geneva, March 15th to April 23rd 2004. On this, the German Foundation for World Population issued the following press release (www.weltbevoelkerung.de/presse texte.html):

UN confirms human right on family planning
The EU parliament decides too:
Every human being is entitled to education and birth control.

Geneva/Hanover/Strasbourg, April 26, 2004.

The Human Rights Commission of the United Nations has acknowledged the human right to health, including the right to education and birth control with an overwhelming majority. The resolution granting every human being the right to reproductive self-determination was passed against one single dissenting vote. The United States were the only nation voting against the resolution.

"It is a question of survival for millions of people in developing countries to be able to protect themselves against HIV / Aids and unintentional pregnancies, and receive the respective health care," explains Renate Bähr, vice director of the German Foundation for World Population (DSW). "The position of the US for us is incomprehensible." (...)

By denying them the right to reproductive self-determination, great harm is caused to hundreds of millions of people and their children; it is a disaster for many women in many countries, their children and families. And it goes without saying that in this way, the development perspectives of whole countries and regions of the world are nullified.

The **fundamentalist opposition**, particularly of influential powers from the "bible belt" in the US, is the underlying reason why the UN Millennium Development Goals address the issue of demographic development less clearly and openly than the situation factually requires. Instead, they (only) refer to goals like the reduction of child mortality, education and equal rights for women, which are positively correlated with the enforcement of reproductive rights. If addressing this issue directly continued to be difficult, in the context of the

Global Marshall Plan Initiative, it would be particularly important for the majority of judicious donor countries to provide for a broader incorporation of respective programs into the international development cooperation. Possible means could be national support programs or, e.g., measures taken in the context of transferring Special Drawing Rights from the IMF (see below) - if the aspired development goals were to be reached until 2015 at all.

What is the state of affairs concerning environmental standards?

Some argue that, from a legal perspective, **all global environmental contracts are already mandatory for the WTO** today [77], a perception largely regarded with scepticism or seen as not sufficiently tested. This proposal for a Global Marshall Plan would render such uncertainty obsolete by explicitly incorporating adherence to these standards into the WTO regulatory frameworks. But what would this implicate for the US, if a Global Marshall Plan is passed and they still refuse to ratify the Kyoto Protocol, which by then should be in force? Such details need to be addressed if a Planetary Contract is to become reality. The question of how to organize the integration of multiple global regimes into a **coherent global governance system** represents a sizable intellectual challenge. Experts will be called for, because a convincing design will be crucial for reaching a consensus on a Global Marshall Plan.

A particularly urgent issue to be addressed in such a contract is adequately safeguarding the livelihoods of those among the poorest, whose survival and well-being depends directly on an **intact natural habitat** from the destructive grasp of world economy (e.g. building of dams or resource degradation without adequate accompanying social measures). This is elaborated on in [97]. In practice this means that, at the very least, appropriate compensations accompanying forced relocation must be provided on a national level. If necessary, adherence or non-adherence would have to be checked and sanctioned by the proposed **legal institute of the global governance systems** to be established, and thus indirectly by WTO jurisdiction.

Interestingly in this context, NGOs and churches are engaged in a discussion similar to that in [97] regarding rich countries' obligations according to the International Covenant on **Economic, Social and Cultural Rights** [139]. Whenever obligations are inferred from this covenant concerning co-financing, e.g. the fight against hunger, the rich countries usually argue in a reserved manner.

Rightfully, NGOs counter this by pointing out that if the rich countries refuse to raise additional funds for development, they are at least by international law restrained from lending financial support to worldwide measures which deprive local populations of the most basic of these rights. In detail, this applies to support measures for exports, e.g. related to construction of dams, mining projects, and possibly agriculture and fisheries, whenever sufficient **accompanying measures ensuring balance and compensation for those adversely affected by such "development projects" are not in place**. By lending such support, the rich North actively harms many poorer people. This can no longer be accepted in the future, and should be impossible as a matter of principle within the framework of a Global Marshall Plan.

It should not go unnoticed that these issues are already addressed today when international development projects are being assessed and funded. Such assessments are **standard procedure before granting credits by the World Bank**. Pertaining to this, **Maartje van Putten** remarks on the so-called "**Equator Principles**" [80]:

> "The Equator Principles are an initiative of today 20 leading Private Banks (such as Credit Suisse Group, ABN-AMRO Bank, Dresdner Bank, City Group, Barclays plc, Royal Bank of Canada). The 20 banks together cover, according to information given to me, in their private lending activities around 80 % of lending for the private sector to developing countries. These principles commit signatory banks to follow the environmental and social safeguard policies set out by the International Finance Corporation (IFC) of the World Bank group. Since this is an initiative concerning the private sector financial activities, this could be taken into account in the Global Marshall Plan."

***Maartje van Putten** [80]*

When it comes to concrete implementation, however, decisions are being based on statements from the respective government. And more often than not, the situation of the people concerned, e.g. concerning resettlement, is quite different in reality than on paper. For this reason, it is of vital importance to grant affected people the **legal means of verification and the right to file actions on the global governance level** to be established. Incidentally, the World Bank has convened a respective **Inspection Panel** in acknowledgement of this issue, and addresses it in its strategy for the interaction with civil society organizations [119]. As a member of this Inspection Panel, Maartje van Putten offers these interesting cues [80]:

> "The World Bank was indeed the first international institution that created in 1993 an independent forum to private citizens that believe they are harmed or could be harmed by a project financed by the World Bank, by the creation of the so called Inspection Panel, a three-member body. This experience of ten years could be of use when a European initiative is taken to set up an international judicial body."

***Maartje van Putten** [80]*

Furthermore, she questions the role of other international development banks:

> "A question not answered is also what the other International Financial Institutions or Development Banks could do. As there are: The Asian Development Bank (ADB), the Inter-American Development Bank (IDB), the European Bank for Reconstruction and Development (EBRD), and the African Development Bank."

***Maartje van Putten** [80]*

Finally, **local governments** in many cases would have to **make a substantially bigger effort on good national governance** than they do today, as a part of the required standards. Only subject to this condition will these countries be eligible for funding by a Planetary Contract, according to the terms of this proposal. Agreements on transition periods allowing for **institutional adjustment measures** and **capacity building** are advisable, similar to the **candidate status** of the EU enlargement processes. For decisions on who is eligible to receive funds, and also with regard to experience with the EU **structural funds**, the following remark by **Maartje van Putten** [80] can be important:

***Maartje van Putten** [80]*

> "Finally I want to pose the question who will benefit from the funds? As is clear from the document, the created funds have to be used to close the gap between the rich and the poor worldwide. The present activities of development institutions are mostly based on the OESO-DAC norms. Certain countries are considered to be developing countries, others belong to the developed world. Yet this division is not accurate anymore. Poverty and even hunger as we know exist also inside Europe and the United States. To get global support for the Initiative might go faster if this phenomenon is recognized. I am aware this creates the problem or risk that the funds will be used more easily in places where other national funds should be in place. Nevertheless, at least recognition of the gap in all places seems to be important. After all, this hidden poverty could create the same risks as we see elsewhere."

If all this takes place in the manner characteristic for the EU enlargement processes, the relatively high growth potentials of countries catching up afford promising perspectives for the abolishment of poverty [78]. As a side effect, a higher **social and cultural balance** will be created on this earth, a step long overdue. These growth potentials could be met in a manner consistent with global sustainability concerns regarding environmental damage and resource consumption, if we manage to create an adequate regulatory framework, if entrepreneurship, good administration and judicature are massively promoted, and if all this is co-financed. On the part of the developed countries, **further, orchestrated opening of**

markets is indispensable. On part of the countries catching up, certain "sealing-off" measures may be temporarily necessary (and the WTO should become more flexible towards this). It may also not be practicable to request entirely democratic conditions from the very beginning. The history of states like **Singapore, Taiwan, Korea or China**, as well as many more among the countries that are rich today, may exemplify this.

At the same time, world contracts in the context described have to provide for the restriction of worldwide resource consumption and environmental pollution, e.g. through **internalization of the real cost into price structures**, in order to steer the growth needed towards sustainability, and to promote respective **technological innovations** and **new ways of living**.

Therefore, the **worldwide protection of the environment** subject to globally agreed conditions is indispensable for the approach taken here. The further **technological progress**, vital for tackling the problems ahead, can thus be directed towards a **substantially increased rate of dematerialization** (**Factor 4 / Factor 10 concepts**) [10, 11]. Key to this is the development of products and manufacturing processes which allow materials to flow in biological and technical cycles.

> "The industrialized countries pursue protectionist policies while preaching free and fair world trade."

Kofi Annan [4]

By applying these structure conditions as requested, the aforementioned **rebound effects** [73, 87] of technological progress can also be avoided. A worldwide social balance, as has been accomplished in Europe, should be possible in the long run through asymmetrical growth rates, which could amount to six to ten percent for many years in the South, while more than two percent will hardly be possible in the

North [69, 87]. However, this will depend on adequate co-financing measures targeted particularly at the establishment of appropriate **national conditions**, including **Good Governance** and a **sufficient social balance**. **More balance is thus a topic to be dealt with both between states and, in many cases, within states**. The **10~> 4:34 concept** of a worldwide social balance developed in [86, 87] emphasizes this notion. Developments of this sort are of essential concern for the proposal of a Global Marshall Plan / Planetary Contract at hand.

Financial support must be linked to explicit obligations. Corruption and capital exodus have to be fought and, where possible, eliminated. It is crucial that solutions in favor of development are supported and rewarded. Above all, the socio-economic development from below has to be promoted (micro credits, agriculture, support of women, education programs, health, involvement of NGOs). Education and training, especially of women, are key factors.

The employment of funds requires a new logic

A third dimension is crucial for a Global Marshall Plan, on top of a **coherent system of governance** (with an anchor role for the WTO), further opening of markets, as well as sufficient **financial resources** and **intellectual contributions**: namely, a **new and improved way of employing funds**. To enable development is not easy. **Good will and money are not enough**, a lesson learned through painful experience of the last decades. The concepts of development assistance have been markedly improved during the last years, and both IMF and World Bank have developed a variety of new approaches. Yet, despite these improvements, employment of the funds for international development, additionally raised through a Global Marshall Plan / Planetary Contract, must follow a **new logic**. It is not our intention to extend the scale of current inter-governmental development assistance, although it will continue to play a role. New approaches can draw from a wealth of experiences from the last years and decades, which have by now made an impact in science, too (ref. [39]).

The concepts of the **new development economics** imply important consequences for development policies and cooperation. They dismiss the unrealistic basic assumptions of the neoclassicist model of competition and take into consideration market power, spill-overs, incomplete information, institutional frameworks, and the problematic implementation of advice in political processes. Corresponding to the increasingly complex nature of the problems faced, the traditional model is not to be replaced by a single new model, but by various theoretical approaches, offering new angles. The **new growth and foreign trade theory, new economic geography, new political economics** and the **new institutional economics** are prominent examples for this new approach. They stand the test particularly in the area of research on developing countries, where the unrealistic traditional assumptions on perfect markets and an optimized functioning of political transmission mechanisms proved to be especially unrealistic (ref. [39]).

Regarding implementation, the design should include **bottom up approaches** as practiced by the **Grameen Bank** and the **micro-credit movement** [145] as well as comprehensive considerations like those by **H. de Soto** [17] concerning **creation of property in poorer countries**, or those of **Amartya Sen** [104], Nobel Prize laureate in economics, on overcoming poverty by enabling initiatives of those concerned. Other valuable sources for questions of design are the reflections by Nobel Prize laureate in economics **Joseph E. Stiglitz** [115], and by **Jean Ziegler** [146], UN Special Rapporteur on the Right to Food, whose statements are further substantiated by his deep personal insights into IMF and World Bank processes.

As **R. K. Stappen** elaborates in a statement on the Global Marshall Plan Initiative [112], all considerations as well as the employment of new funds must be embedded into the **Rio and Johannesburg follow-up processes**. The further development can be based on the **Agenda 21** model with its far reach into the future as a framework for action. These agendas are scheduled for a larger international review in 2016/2017. In this sense, a Global Marshall Plan would be a continuation of the Agenda 21. Additional funds should accordingly be employed for the enhancement of the **Global Environment Facility**.

P. Johnston [53] maintains that the conditions for **foreign investment** in developing countries should be improved. This area holds a large potential for development, particularly if principles of **Corporate Social Responsibility** are adhered to. Today, **money transfers by remittances of emigrants** back into their home countries have a higher volume than the international development assistance, and have multiple positive effects. Financial support must be steered towards **adjusted new structures compliant with sustainability concerns**; to copy the unsustainable structures of the North cannot be an objective. Instead, **growth and resource consumption must be uncoupled**. Therefore, the **transfer of knowledge and technology** instead of money may play an important role.

Of strong interest, but also highly disputed, are new developments concerning the proprietorship of software, e.g. **open source**. In this context, **W. Heidrich** describes another interesting initiative in the field of **innovation culture**, utilizing the possibilities of the internet [43]. The approach proposed here could efficiently merge the innovative factors - knowledge pertaining to new technologies, human resources, scientific-technical infrastructures, and knowledge on how innovative processes evolve.

A standardized global **platform for innovative technologies** (http:\\ibitz.biz), built from autonomous regional professional exchange sites, will offer new possibilities for regional economic development if local future-oriented structures are consequently used in connection with networks of innovation-oriented experts. The creation of such a network is in preparation. New global innovative partnerships based on the **application of creative work** and making "**special use of scientific-technical infrastructures**" are capable of significantly increasing the potential for innovations and thus spur the economic development of regions both in the South and the North of the globe. A precondition is that the people actively involved receive a fair share of the economic success, and initial investment is minimized. Allowing space for innovative and entrepreneurial action, granting tax incentives for "work invested in innovation processes," and making "special use of scientific-technical infrastructures" are factors (according to considerations from **W. Heidrich**) capable of significantly boosting the development of a global innovation culture which is based on a "**creative laborism**" and the change of the current market economy towards a socio-ecological market economy within the framework of a Global Marshall Plan.

Mobilizing citizens could provide ample opportunity, **M. Gege** [29] maintains, e.g. through **public funds** geared to promote sustainability. The application and promotion of such funds could be an effective mechanism for further **leveraging** funds we hope to activate within the scope of the Global Marshall Plan. Concerning the usage of co-financing means, **P. Hesse** of the Peter-Hesse-Foundation explains [45]:

***Peter Hesse** [45]*

> "The co-financing of an adequate conduct of states provided in the concept of a Global Marshall Plan, for the establishment of and adherence to social and environmental standards, may prove effective in cases where the respective governments successfully aspire "good governance," i.e. a transparent and efficient administration, but not in states with corrupt regimes. Therefore, effective poverty reduction and basic social services often cannot be achieved via governmental channels - although this should be an obligation of the state."

Peter Hesse
[45]

Direct means must then be found for enabling the people directly concerned to help themselves. To achieve this, transparency and control are required, as well as people - mediators, facilitators - honestly committed to working at and for the grass-root level. Such people can and should be found directly in the respective countries, close to and with the cultural competence to facilitate the self-help of needy populations. This must however be supplemented by trustworthy donor deputies managing the transfer of funds from outside to the people concerned.

P. Hesse refers in this context particularly to the positive experiences of the concept "**Partnership Helper Model**" developed with his collaboration, and its continuations.

Further necessities must be pointed out here. It is imminent to improve the worldwide status of information on various **socio-economic parameters**, linked with **digitalized cartographic information**. This topic is known under the term of **Digital Earth** [60, 61], and has been significantly inspired by former US vice-president **Al Gore**, as has been the Global Marshall Plan Initiative [36]. It will require much more attention if the conditions for a sustainable development are to be established. At any rate, first steps have been made and can be built on. In particular, existing means of collecting and providing information via satellite, e.g., must be made available not solely for **military and security purposes** but also for the promotion of a sustainable development. To this end, the European satellite radio navigation system **Galileo** opens new potentials.

Further reference shall be made to the comprehensive reflections of **George Soros** [109], who proposes that private initiatives compete against each other for the funds allocated for co-financing. A respective neutral jury should be instituted within the IMF, but its allocations should be materially independent of the IMF's decision structures.

It is equally important to recognize the need for an **adjusted technology**, which has been widely observed. Obviously, to transplant the **large-scale technologies** of rich countries into developing countries is not always an adequate solution. Rather, technologies should be adjusted to the particular circumstances, focussing on **generating employment** and the gradual individual development of billions of relatively poor people. **Agriculture** will continue to play an important role for a long time [142]. **Renewable Energies**, help towards self-help, decentralized approaches, and the **development of self-initiative** are major topics.

We also have to see to it that the **financial means employed reach the local people** to the highest possible extent [77, 78, 79, 106, 107, 109, 139], instead of being largely used up by experts from rich countries managing projects on site, as is very often the case today. Practices can no longer be acceptable where more than 50 percent and sometimes even up to 90 percent of current development assistance remain in the donor country.

III. Objectives: The Global Marshall Plan Initiative as an Intermediate Step towards Sustainable Global Conditions

With the United Nations Millennium Development Goals, the world community has established a clear notion on the progress to be made by 2015 in terms of eradicating poverty and destitution. Simultaneously, the Zedillo Report identifies the financial dimensions of this endeavor as well as the implementation mechanisms required. Now is the time to implement this program.

The concept of the Global Marshall Plan Initiative uses the objective of implementing the **UN Millennium Development Goals** (www.un.org/milleniumgoals) as an intermediate step towards the establishment of an Eco-Social Market Economy, with these internationally accepted goals functioning as a benchmark scheduled for 2015. They constitute an ambitious project that has been verified internationally, and has given rise to conceptions of the **additional funds required** that will likely be met with international approval, and to new ideas for their practical implementation which have been outlined at the end of chapter II. Thus, the conditions are favorable. Now is the time to proceed from the proclamation of goals to their implementation, and to results. This is the objective of the **Global Marshall Plan / Planetary Contract Initiative.**

The UN Millennium Development Goals

Until 2015, the UN Millennium Development Goals include the following objectives:

- **Fight against extreme poverty and hunger:** the number of people worldwide who earn less than one Dollar per day is to be reduced by half (more than one billion people today).

The current report by the Food and Agriculture Organization (FAO) in Rome clearly indicates that the number of starving people does not decline but is again on the rise, i.e. the world is farther than ever from reaching the Millennium Development Goals 25,. Substantial progress has been virtually restricted to the positive development in China and, partly, in India, comprising approximately 2.3 billion people.

- **Education** for all: Ensure that all boys and girls complete a full course of primary schooling.

- **Fight against child mortality:** Reduce child mortality to one third of current numbers.

- **Improve maternal health:** Substantial improvements are required. This topic relates to questions of Reproductive Health, and thus to demographic development (e.g. Child Spacing) as mentioned above.

- **Combat HIV/AIDS, Malaria and other diseases:** This is a major concern for some of the least developed countries facing medical states of emergency. The goal is to bring to a halt or even reverse the current spreading of HIV/AIDS and the incidence of Malaria and other worldwide diseases.

- **Ensure environmental sustainability:** Amongst other things, the loss of environmental resources should be reversed, the number of people without access to safe drinking water (more than one billion today) halved by 2015, and by 2020 the living conditions of more than 100 million people living in slums significantly improved.

- **Develop** a global partnership for development: Develop further an **open trading and financial system** including a commitment to **Good Governance**, development and poverty reduction - nationally and internationally.

- Address the least developed countries' special needs including enhanced debt relief for heavily indebted poor countries.

- **Develop decent and productive work for youth**. In cooperation with pharmaceutical companies, provide access to affordable essential drugs in developing countries.

- In cooperation with the private sector, make available the benefits of new technologies – especially information and communications technologies, thus contributing to bridging the **digital divide**.

(Note: as to the digital divide, ref. [27, 33, 48, 57, 99, 144], as to the abolishment of child labor, ref. [52]).

Drawing from preparatory work dating as far back as 1986 [4, 20, 26, 55, 105, 118, 123, 124, 125, 126, 128, 140, 141] the UN Millennium Development Goals have been concerted on UN level. Meanwhile, these goals have been agreed upon by major international organizations like the WTO, ILO, World Bank, or IMF, as well as the OECD and all large nation states. The **world has codified what it aspires to achieve in the medium-term in its fight against poverty** – assuming that such statements are sincere and not just noncommittal instruments to gain time and to hold off on actions.

The Millennium Goals are truly ambitious. Thus UN Secretary General Kofi Annan recently pointed out that, starting today, 150,000 people per day would have to be connected to a water system in order to achieve the respective goal until 2015. We are nowhere near this stage. As always, the unsettled question is how to ensure that goals set in a major international statement will be effectively achieved. Once again, no substantial progress has been made with any of the objectives pompously declared. The British Chancellor of the Exchequer Gordon Brown, who **follows the topic with particular global dedication and vision**, recently delivered an impressively precise and clear comment on the situation in an important contribution for the conference „Making Globalisation Work For All – The Challenge Of Delivering The Monterrey Consensus", held in London on February 16, 2004 [13]. On this occasion, he also elaborated on his proposal of an **International Finance Facility**, which has been taken up by many in the meantime, albeit lacking clearness as to how the funds will factually be raised, which may turn out as its major pitfall in the author's view. In his contribution, which repeatedly alludes to the historical Marshall Plan, Gordon Brown says (citations picked and highlighted by the author of this text):

- *2005 is a crucial, defining year; a year of challenge but also a year of opportunity.*

- *Five years before, in a historic declaration - in perhaps the most significant international commitment of recent decades - every world leader, every major international body, almost every single country, signed up to the historic shared task of meeting over fifteen years eight Millennium Development Goals - an extraordinary plan to definitively right some of the great wrongs of our time. At the heart of which is a clear commitment to ensuring education for every child, the elimination of avoidable infant and maternal deaths, and the halving of poverty.*

- *Next year, 2005, is the first date that the first target comes due.*

- *But we know already that the first target to be set and to be met - the 2005 target that ensures for girls the same opportunities in primary and secondary education as boys - is going to be missed. Not only are the vast majority - 60 per cent of developing countries - unlikely to meet the target but most of these are, on present trends, unlikely to achieve this gender equality for girls even by 2015. This is not good enough - this is not the promise that we made.*

- *Take education. Yes, in the past decade, primary enrolments have increased at twice the rate of the 1980s. But consider the 115 million children - 80 million boys and girls in Africa and south and west Asia - who did not go to school this Monday morning.*

- *To reach our education goals requires 80 million new primary school places in Africa alone over the coming decade and at the current rate of progress more than 70 countries will fail to achieve universal primary education by our target date, and in Sub-Saharan Africa we will not achieve what we committed to by 2015 until at the earliest 2129. This is not good enough - the promise we made was for 2015 not 2129.*

- *And take our Millennium global poverty target. Although the number of people living in extreme poverty has fallen by 10 per cent in the last ten years, there are one billion people still living on less than $1 a day. And without greatly increased growth, Sub-Saharan Africa, the Middle East, North Africa, Latin America, the Caribbean and the transition economies of Europe and Central Asia will all fail to see the halving of their poverty by 2015. Our best estimate is that it will not be achieved in Sub Saharan Africa for more than a hundred years. This is not good enough - the dream we dreamed was not for 2147 but for 2015.*

- *Too often our world has set targets like our Millennium Development Goals and failed to meet them so that a global target is only a measure of how far we have failed not succeeded.*

- *Too often we have set goals, reset them, and recalibrated them again so that all we end up doing is mitigating the extent to which we have failed.*

- *And if we, knowing what we have to do, fail to act now, we will not only fail the poor this time but they will never believe our promises again.*

- *Let us be clear: the world did not come together in New York in 2000, come together in Doha in 2001 and come together in Johannesburg and Monterrey in 2002 to make promises and then walk by on the other side when we see them broken.*

- *So when the need is pressing, when it is our generation that has made historic commitments, the simple questions that, to use the words of an American President, we must ask are:*

If not now – when?
If not us, who?
If not together, how?

- *Not left to some other time and some other people but now and us, working together.*

- *And I propose we all - all of us who believe that globalisation must also mean justice on a global scale - commit ourselves to a specific course of action, and then each of us as partners - government, business, NGOs and faith groups, international institutions – agree to work together to make the radical changes required. And as Tony Blair has said: for the sake of Africa and the poorest countries we will make our 2005 G8 presidency a 'Development Presidency'.*

- *Put simply, our proposal is that in return for developing countries developing their own country owned, community owned poverty reduction plans to expand their own development, investment and trade, and eliminate corruption:*

  - *we, the richest countries, commit the $10 billion needed each year for education for all.*

  - *we, the richest countries, release at least $10 billion for tackling AIDS, TB, and malaria.*

  - *we finance sustainable debt relief.*

  - *we finance, for the poorest countries, the building of capacity to trade and that we do so by increasing development aid, on the road to 0.7 per cent of GDP, and by, immediately, creating an International Finance Facility that, by leveraging in an additional $50 billion each year until 2015, brings forward the development aid and investment that is essential to meet the Millennium Goals.*

- *The richest countries making a commitment to provide long-term, predictable and effective aid as investment to the countries that need it most, and promising every developing country that is prepared to make the reforms necessary that they will not be denied the resources for their own country-owned, community-owned programmes to tackle illiteracy, disease and destitution.*

- *While the scale of the new deal we propose between developed countries and developing countries is massive, the demand we make is not unprecedented. Let us remember that to finance the development of a ravaged* *post war Europe, the richest country in the world - the USA - agreed in the historic Marshall Plan of 1948 to transfer one per cent of their national income each and every year for four years - a transfer in total of the equivalent in today's money of $75 billion a year.*

- *This Marshall Plan was a transfer of resources in what was more than an act of charity: it was a frank recognition that - as we say today of the relationship between developed and developing countries - prosperity like peace is indivisible and prosperity to be sustained must be shared.*

- *In setting out his objectives at Harvard University in 1948 Marshall articulated then the greater unifying vision that can inspire us still today of a global fight against, as he said, 'hunger, poverty, desperation and chaos' that would secure not merely 'a working economy throughout the world' but 'permit the emergence of political and social conditions in which free institutions can exist'.*

- *And although today's global new deal would be constructed in new times, it is rooted in the Marshall Plan's enduring values. Like these visionaries we understand that there are global concerns - including terror - to which together we must respond with unified resolution.*

- *Like our predecessors we see the need for a comprehensive plan that can only succeed if it goes beyond temporary relief to wholesale economic development. Like them we see the need for a new global economic and social order grounded in both rights and responsibilities. And so like theirs our proposals ask the poorest countries also to rise to the challenge.*

- *If anything, however, the scale and the global breadth of the challenge is more urgent and pressing today. Even more so than in Marshall's era national safety and global reconstruction are inextricably linked. And even more so than in Marshall's time our interdependence means - as September 11th proved so tragically - that what happens to the poorest citizen in the poorest country can directly affect the richest citizen in the richest country - making the case for visionary action stronger now than it was 50 years ago.*

- *And our vision of the way forward - akin to Marshall's challenge to rich and poor countries alike - is that by each meeting their obligations for change all countries can benefit and the Millennium Goals can be achieved.*

- *For the richest countries: it will mean new responsibilities - to open our markets and to curb protectionism and to transfer resources - but also new opportunities - increased trade and a globalisation that also means both security and justice on a global scale.*

- *For the poorest countries: new responsibilities - to pursue transparent, corruption-free policies for stability and a properly sequenced opening up of investment, trade and economic growth - and new opportunities - with the capacity for increased growth and trade and a transfer of resources from rich to poor to tackle long standing problems of ill-health, illiteracy, poverty and underdevelopment*

- *Making better use of existing aid - reordering priorities, untying aid and pooling funds internationally to release additional funds for the poorest countries - is essential to achieve both value for money and the improved outcomes we seek, but in addition to these reforms, I ask this conference to recognise that aid to Africa which was $33 per person ten years ago is just $20 per person now, that the scale of the resources to tackle AIDS, illiteracy and poverty is indeed in excess of what traditional funding can offer and I therefore ask all governments both to* *move towards our agreed target of 0.7 per cent and to, immediately, look seriously at our proposal for the International Finance Facility.*

- *The IFF is founded upon long-term, binding donor commitments from the richest countries. It builds upon the additional $ 16 billion already pledged at Monterrey. And it leverages in additional money from the international capital markets to raise the amount of development aid for the years to 2015 from $50 billion a year to $ 100 billion per year. $ 50 billion that will allow us to attack the root causes of poverty not just the symptoms, and to meet the Millennium Development Goals.*

So the practical benefits of the IFF are:

- *We could write off more debt and because it will enable us to give grants, ensure a sustainable exit from debt.*

- *On health, we could meet our global goal of cutting infant mortality and maternal mortality and eliminating malaria and TB.*

- *On the AIDS crisis, which Bono has spoken about far more eloquently than I, we could make available treatments and contribute to the search for a vaccine that might permanently end its scourge.*

- *On education, we could make primary schooling for all not just a distant dream but a practical reality.*

- *On trade, because we recognise that to benefit from access to our markets, the poorest countries need investments in infrastructure, education, health and economic development, the IFF could provide the support necessary.*

- *Let us continue to work with you to examine the Tobin tax; the Soros proposal for Special Drawing Rights; other forms of revenue raising on a worldwide basis. But each one of these proposals will come down to one simple question; is there sufficient will in the richest countries to agree these profound changes?*

- *I believe that the advantage of the International Finance Facility I have described is not just that it is a better means of providing the necessary resources immediately and thus far faster than other initiatives, but also that unlike other measures like taxes - where all countries must impose it or it can work for none - the IFF can proceed even if some fail to participate.*

- *I thank the growing number of countries who have indicated support for the IFF, in the G7 and elsewhere. Francis Mer the Finance Minister of France and I will hold, in Paris in April, a conference on the IFF, which 60 countries will attend, and the IMF and World Bank will discuss the conclusions of their report on it later this year.*

- *2015 is the fixed point on our horizon - seemingly distant but closer than we think. But it is actually 2005 - as close as can be - that will determine whether we are likely to make the rest of the journey.*

- *If we let things slip, the Millennium Goals will become just another dream we once had, and we will indeed be sitting back on our sofas and switching on our TVs and - I am afraid - watching people die on our screens for the rest of our lives. We will be the generation that betrayed its own heart.*

- *Last year - 2003 - the world trade talks stalled and we took a step back from 2002. Let us make next year different.*

- *I appeal to business - whom I thank for their attendance today: to engage with the development challenge - participating in a dialogue that I am confident will lead eventually to a richer world.*

- *And I appeal to NGOs and faith groups: to hold us accountable, to be the conscience of the world, to be the voice that guides us at this crucial crossroads, to work together with no one ever subordinating their own objectives but recognising that each of our objectives can be better realised if we can agree the financing to underpin them.*

In 2015 we cannot look back and say:
"It was not us who acted, it had to be left to the next generation; It was not now, but some other distant time in the future" - That is not good enough

- *When the need is urgent and our responsibilities clear; and even when the path ahead is difficult, hard, and long, let us not lose hope but have the courage in our shared resolve to find the will to act. And let us say to each other in the words of Isaiah "though you were wearied by the length of your way, you did not say it was hopeless - you found new life in your strength".*

- *The strength together to fight poverty, remove destitution, end illiteracy, cure disease. The challenge is for our time and for our generation. And let us achieve it together.*

Gordon Brown's text is wonderful. Let's hope that the British G8 presidency in 2005, designated as **"Development Presidency"**, will get the implementation of the topical concerns up to speed. A glass halfway filled is either half-full or half-empty. The author and many observers from NGOs view the results achieved since 2000 more critical than Gordon Brown puts them, i.e. mainly as dashed hopes. Neither the 2002 World Summit on Financing for Development in Monterrey, Mexico, nor the **Rio+10 Earth** Summit in Johannesburg, 2002, or, finally, the **WTO development** round in Cancun in 2003 have effectuated the results hoped for, as far as the global civil society is concerned. The data accumulated for the current world development report [25] indicate clearly the aforementioned fact that in the last years, instead of being eradicated, hunger is on the rise again. As is often the case, major deficits prevail concerning both **funding** and **implementation mechanisms** in this context. This is where the Initiative for a Global Marshall Plan / Planetary Contract takes up.

***Kofi Annan**, October 2000 [4]*

"The heads of state and government have declared to free their peoples from thescourge of war, from bitter and inhumane poverty and from the threats to life caused by environmental pollution and lack of resources on our planet. They have committed themselves to promote democracy and rule of law, to protect our children and other endangered groups and to pay special attention to the needs of the African continent. They have also promised to grant the United Nations an instrument for the implementation of all these goals with more effectiveness.

These promises give us hope but they will not make a change if they are not followed by deeds. Shortly after the Millennium Summit, the blood shed in the Near East illustrated how dangerous it can be if there is no solution for political and social misery."

According to an analysis by the UN (the **2001 Zedillo Report**, ref. www.un.org/reports/financing/full_report.pdf), approximately US$ 50 billion in co-financing funds are lacking per year for the achievement of the UN Millennium Development Goals. An additional US$ 20 billion per year are needed for the provision of **(global) public goods.** For a correct perspective on the dimension of these missing funds, please note that the scale of international **development assistance is about US$ 56 Billion** per year. This amount represents an important statistic for the Millennium Development Goal "Establishment of a global Partnership for Development" and has **declined** from 0.33 % of the donor countries' gross domestic product in 1999 to 0.22 % in 2001. Where the poorest countries are concerned, the decline is even more serious, namely from 0.09 % to 0.05 %.

Particularly depressing is the extremely low contribution of the world's richest country, additionally constricted by numerous requirements, of merely 0.11 % by now (including recent increases) [124], while **Europe's contribution of about 0.35 percent GDP** adds up to a **total of 70 % of global development assistance** today. The level of international development assistance is much too low and has to be **increased quickly and drastically**, eventually reaching the 0.7 % promised for decades. This is one of the core demands of the Global Marshall Plan Initiative, which would make a major contribution to this end, if its objectives were implemented.

Furthermore, the volume of development assistance of US$ 56 billion has to be compared to the interest **payments of the South to the North**, which amount to about US$ 136 billion per year. In comparison, Germany's governmental budgets currently amount to approximately 1000 billion Euros. The current US military budget is about US$ 440 billion, and in November 2003, the US congress has given approval for a further **US$ 87.5 billion to fund the military operations in Iraq and Afghanistan** in 2004. A mere **US$ 18.6 billion** of this are designated for **humanitarian aid** and reconstruction in Iraq, and US$ 1.2 billion for reconstruction in Afghanistan. Of the reconstruction funds for Iraq, US$ 5.6 billion are designated for repairing the electrical power grid, US$ 4.3 billion for water and sewage systems, US$ 3.2 billion for the establishment of security and law enforcement, and US$ 1.9 billion for the restoration of the oil infrastructure.

From the point of view of this text, these funds spent on civil projects now and in the future could be completely or partially deducted from the **US contribution to a Global Marshall Plan**. For instance, they could replace the US's obligation of fulfilling special drawing right quotas for worldwide development to the IMF, as will be explained later in this text. The corresponding special drawing rights would then increase the US currency reserves.

IV. Prospects of a Global Marshall Plan

The Marshall Plan as role model: The efforts the US made for Europe's reconstruction after World War II were fuelled by the realization that to stabilize Europe was essential for global security. The need for an extensive stabilization on a global level is even more pressing today. The circumstances may be different, but the spirit of the Marshall Plan is in urgent demand again, as basis for a Planetary Contract.

After World War II, the US supported **Europe's reconstruction** by implementing a **Marshall Plan**. Besides **opening their markets to a large extent for European products**, the US employed substantial sums during four years, amounting on average to 1.3 % of the US gross domestic product, and up to 2 % in top periods. This large investment was made subject to the **establishment of democratic and market economy structures**, and proved to be a major determinant of the quick boom in Europe, especially in Germany. Its success was based on the establishment of order and stability, and the usage of the specific motivational and economic potentials resulting from the extreme breakdown during the war. At the same time, this effort on part of the US inspired **courage and hope** in the people of Europe, going a long way beyond the purely financial part. The Marshall Plan turned out to be a sagacious investment **for the US too**, and facilitated an **economic miracle** in Europe.

Kofi Annan* *[4]

"Within the United Nations we are jointly fighting to eliminate AIDS and other epidemics, to control climate change and to make clean air and water available to all. Within the United Nations we fight for a global market which is beneficial for all of us and which enables the poor to free themselves from poverty. Economic growth has to be promoted, but the fruits of this growth have to be distributed more broadly."

In these difficult times, we should tie up to this encouraging historical experience. There is an urgent need for a dedicated and rapid promotion of **global development under the**

terms of sustainability. This is the goal of a Global Marshall Plan / Planetary Contract. Europe in particular is capable to, and must also play a key role in this process by providing the framework for an international forum working towards the development of an Eco-Social Global Marshall Plan. It goes without saying that the global conditions and plights today bear little resemblance to the situation after World War II (e.g. as regards educational standards, historical experience, political system, economic basis, infrastructure, cultural background, etc.) and that, in many ways, other procedures are called for now than at the time of the first Marshall Plan. It is the **fundamental principle** that can be carried forward, not the details. In particular, the time frames for implementation (around 50 years) will be very different, and individual countries will develop their very own dynamics [68, 87], which must be taken into account. Thus, there is no need for quick solutions, but for **stamina**, far beyond the year 2015.

Despite or even because of this, a substantial effect could be produced if the rich part of the world would now introduce serious efforts for development, a visible signal of solidarity, a large investment of also an **emotional**, **intellectual nature**. The chances for such an effect are even better because this investment would be connected to the **establishment of reliable regulatory structures**, benefiting both the North and the South. It could be the foundation of a **global economic miracle**. The world could be much more wealthy than it is today [78]. Under the conditions of a Global Marshall Plan / Planetary Contract, the **global domestic product** could be increased **ten-fold** within 50 to 100 years. This increase could be four-fold in the North, and 34-fold in the South, accomplishing a global social balance as can be observed in Europe today, while technological progress would protect the environment. The latter topic is elaborated in the author's considerations on his **future formula 10~> 4:34** [86, 87]. Without fail, such a step would implicate a – relatively speaking – **massively dematerialized** gross global product and respective **change of lifestyles**, resulting from changed price relations, amongst other things. Concerning the **prospects of such a path**: the chances for the implementation of a Global Marshall Plan / Planetary Contract are better now than at any stage during the last years, despite all international blockades. This is due to the following developments, amongst other things:

> The global resource exhaustion, particularly by the "rich North", is already threatening sustainability and calls for measures binding future growth to a dramatic increase in resource efficiency (technological progress and a change in life styles), and for an orientation towards closed-loop material cycles.

1.) The **market fundamentalist model of globalization** has largely lost credit, and for good reason, e.g.:

- The failure of the New Economy, the bouncing of the "Financial Bubble", and the outrageous acts of fraud committed by insiders on international financial markets that surfaced with it [85, 87, 108, 109].

- The disastrous effect of market fundamentalism in Russia, contrasted by the much more positive development in China.

- The mounting divide between the poor and the rich on this globe.

- The increasingly sterile and "mendacious" system of concepts and media reporting (honest communication being replaced by public awareness management and political correctness), which causes many to stop listening altogether.

- The events of September 11, 2001 and the insufficient political response, the consequences of which become increasingly apparent in Iraq and in Israel/Palestine [49, 65, 87].

- The dramatic increase in global environmental degradation.

It is indeed time for a new approach [9, 59, 135].

2.) The **WTO conference in Cancun 2003** has very nearly stalled all further development of the WTO. The erosion of this important international organization is imminent, and would result in a relapse into bilateral agreements, detrimental for weaker countries and bearing incalculable consequences [87]. This must be considered against a background of a brutalization of conventions on all sides, accumulating into a climate of hate, terrorism, and, in part, actions breaching international law, further augmenting aggressions. A new approach that offers perspectives for the future must be adopted rapidly. The need for new ways has been reconfirmed at the end of 2003 in Geneva, when the **World Summit on the Information Society (WSIS)** again revealed the **conflict between North and South**, in this case concerning the **Digital Divide**.

3.) The proposal of a Global Marshall Plan ties up to the **great achievement of the US** after World War II. Despite the aforementioned incomparableness of the situations, this could prove psychologically beneficial. It has also been mentioned that at all WTO negotiations, the US (pressured by environmentalists and unions) and the other developed countries have demanded **adherence to environmental** and particularly **to core ILO standards**. The developed countries now have the chance to accomplish this advancement of the WTO that they have **declared as their goal** repeatedly and publicly, by connecting it to a Global Marshall Plan. It may however become apparent instead that these demands have been shammed by some, or that the willingness to contribute to their implementation through co-financing is lacking. It may also result in a new dissociation between Europe and the US, or between "Old Europe" and others. Let us hope that none of this will happen. But even if it does, the resulting clarity would be better for future discussions about the world order than the inefficient "state of suspense" of arguments prevalent today.

In any case, to a substantial extent, the Initiative for a Global Marshall Plan / Planetary Contract should be linked to the implementation of certain standards, at the very least to those pertaining directly to objectives of the UN Millennium Development Goals. The **prohibition of child labor** in all transactions covered by the WTO would be such a case, if by 2015 school **education for all children in this world will finally be guaranteed and funded by both the world community and the respective local governments**.

4.) The sporadic evaluative differences between **continental Europe and Great Britain**, e.g. concerning free trade, do not exist here. As has been stated above, it was the British **Chancellor of the Exchequer Gordon Brown** who, at the Rio+10-Earth Summit in Johannesburg in July/August 2002 (www.globalpolicy.org/socecon/ffd/2002/1216brown.htm), made the proposition of a Global Marshall Plan in this spirit, if not the detailed terms described here. He has reconfirmed this in the exceedingly important document that has been cited above [13], and with his additional statement that the British government will use its G8 presidency in 2005 as a **Development Presidency**.

5.) In some **Latin American states**, the population protested against the erroneous trends of market fundamentalist approaches in recent months, which has raised concerns. These protests have finally made it plain to many global players in the rich countries that certain forms of "exploitation" of the poorer people in poorer countries (particularly following the implementation of the original Washington Consensus [56]) will no longer be practicable with guaranteed high yields; in spite of being internationally accepted today through the exploitation of free market concepts and the interaction between the local elites and the elites in the North.

6.) Because it is obvious that the approaches presently taken are ill-suited for overcoming poverty and establishing sustainable conditions, WTO, IWF and WB work on new approaches to manage the global challenges, in different contexts and in one case in interaction with the **Club of Rome**. Some of their current reflections have been incorporated into this text.

7.) Meanwhile, many **prominent persons** have argued for a Global Marshall Plan, e.g. the **former foreign minister, Hans-Dietrich Genscher**, from the German liberal party whose position carries special authority in this context (please refer to the **Declaration of Stuttgart**, its circle of first signatories, relevant press releases at www.globalmarshallplan.org, as well as to references in the appendix). With the **Federal Association for Business Promotion and Foreign Trade** (president: Carl-Eduard von Bismarck, great-great-grandson of Otto von Bismarck, founder of Germany's social legislation; chairman: Dieter Härthe), the first industrial federation offered its active support for the idea of a Global Marshall Plan on December 4th, 2003.

8.) Thematically, our proposal incorporates considerations of the **Stiftung Weltethos** (World Ethos Foundation, Prof. Dr. Hans Küng) and of the **Open Society Initiative** (George Soros). Similar objectives are targeted by the **World Future Council Initiative** (www.worldfuturecouncil.org).

9.) The **Eco-Social Forum Europe** (president: former Austrian Vice-chancellor Dr. h.c. **Josef Riegler**) promotes the topic. It is regarded as an intermediate step towards a **worldwide Eco-Social Market Economy** [87, 93], a system also favored by, e.g., the Federation of Austrian Industry [76]. **Prince El Hassan of Jordan**, president of the **Club of Rome** and the **Arab Thought Forum**, and many members of the Club (besides the author, these are Wouter van Dieren, Amsterdam, Bohdan Hawrylyshyn, Conches-Geneva, Esko Kalimo, Espoo-Finnland, Sergey Kapitza, Moscow, Pentii Malaska, Helsinki, Mike Mesarovic, Pittsburgh, Uwe Möller, Hamburg, Ivo Slaus, Zagreb, Ernst Ulrich von Weizsäcker, Berlin, Raoul Weiler, Antwerp, Anders Wijkman, Brussels) support the program, as does the **Club of Budapest**. Furthermore, the Initiative directly seizes on contributions made within the last decade by the **Information Society Forum** (ISF) of the European Union (www.europa.eu.int/index-de.htm) [48], the **Information Society Forum/Forum Info 2000 of the German Federal Government** (www.forum-informationsgesellschaft.de/fig/extern) [27], and by the **Global Society Dialogue** (www.global-society-dialogue.org) [33], initiated by the ISF in 1999.

10.) There are strong connections to considerations by Helmut Schmidt and others in the **InterAction Council** of former **heads of state** and government (www.interactioncouncil.org/).

I. Why is there a chance on part of the institutional design to implement a Global Marshall Plan within a few years?

International agreements on goals, standards, funding, implementation, or compliance systems for the organization of global tasks are extremely complex and generally require time frames of ten years and more. Therefore, to implement a Global Marshall Plan Initiative with regard to the year 2015 would be utterly impossible if all this were yet to be accomplished. Fortunately, the situation is much more favorable. All components essential to a Global Marshall Plan already exist; they have been accomplished in the course of the last 10 to 15 years. What is still missing is an adequate linkage of these components.

At this point, an intellectual contribution is called for, a central clue to be found, something like the "Rosetta Stone", which would finally make the translation of the hieroglyphics possible. The formulation of the elements of the solution was the largest contribution to be made; now the existing elements have to be adequately integrated into a coherent, comprehensive system of Global Governance. This shall be the accomplishment of the Global Marshall Plan Initiative.

II. What does already exist?

1. Objectives

To formulate objectives shared by all countries and international organizations is a demanding process. This process was accomplished during the period 1990-2000. The **United Nations Millennium Development** Goals of 2000 present a thoroughly considered list of objectives pertaining to critical global problems, a schedule of accomplishments the world community aspires until 2015. These Millennium Development Goals have been widely accepted and communicated, and many international authorities from all parts of society support these goals. So does the Global Marshall Plan Initiative, interpreting these goals as an intermediate step towards a **worldwide Eco-Social Market Economy.** The latter represents an elaborated political concept with direct connections to European success stories like the EU enlargement processes.

2. Regimes and Organization

To pursue global goals requires **sophisticated regimes** with adequate regulatory frameworks. Their formulation is also a process of decades. Fortunately, elaborate solutions in the form of international contracts and organizations already exist in the fields of trade, finance, social standards, environmental standards, cultural standards, etc.. These are in particular the international regimes like **WTO, IMF/WB, ILO, UNESCO**, and the international environmental agreements supervised by **UNEP**; all these are of high importance today. The listed organizations and contracts are highly developed, and some of them have their own sanction mechanisms, supported by respective legal structures. They are the **core elements of any global regulatory framework for Global Governance**. We are fortunate that they are already in place. What needs to be done is to link these regimes.

3. Instruments of implementation

The world possesses both longstanding experience with **international development cooperation** and the respective organizations. During the last 20 years, a long distance has been covered towards cooperation with **non-governmental organizations** in issues of implementation, and new approaches are continuously incorporated, like the **micro-credit** movement. All these processes and experience can be built upon.

4. Funding instruments and distribution

For decades, a debate has been going on about **international instruments** of funding for development and the volume aspired. A wealth of experience exists on what is possible, and what is not. Of particular interest for raising funds are new instruments **outside of present government budgets.** In this context, using special drawing rights of the IMF, a Tobin tax on international capital transactions, or a tax with regard to Fair Trade have been discussed for a long time, as have been instruments dealing with fair pricing for exploiting scarce resources, or for induced environmental damages, the latter for example in the context of the Kyoto Protocol.

In the light of the considerable funds which shall be internationally generated and used as suggested in this proposal, the assumption of responsibility for the use of funds, especially with reference to the role of international parliaments, has to be thought through carefully. As far as the funds available with the IMF and the World Bank can be distributed, according to internationally agreed standards, this could be done according to already established mechanisms.

This applies in a similar way to the special drawing rights of the IMF, whose generation has to be agreed upon by the governments and parliaments. Furthermore, a consent is needed about the use of these funds in the context of international development aid on national level - or in this case directly on level of the IMF.

At the same time it would have to be fixed to what extent national parliaments and national authorities can be given influence on the concrete use of funds in the sense of economic cooperation and overseas development aid (ODA). These details have to be clarified and further developed by the aimed-for EU advisory board for the design of a Global Marshall Plan. The responsibility for the use of these funds is one of the fundamental elements in the puzzle which has to be solved by the international design for better globalization if the Global Marshall Plan is to be successful.

5. Legal systems

The various regimes are equipped with legal or arbitrational instruments of differing enforcement power, **enabling the settlement of disputes**. They are also equipped with specific **sanction mechanisms** that can be applied.

III. What has yet to be done?

All components essential for a viable global governance system already exist, and there is largely congruency between goals, regimes, financing instruments and options for sanctions. What is missing is the **linkage of these different regimes.** In this context, the natural approach is to integrate core standards of the ILO, UNESCO, and central agreements pertaining to international environmental protection directly into the regulatory frameworks for trade at the WTO, and to make them mandatory for the financing of activities and projects by IMF and World Bank.

A consensus of the community of states is prerequisite to this, especially in the context of the WTO boards. Key to achieving such a consensus will once again be that the rich world **employs adequate volumes of co-financing for development** programs. Once the respective standards are implemented on WTO level, IMF and World Bank will act accordingly and adopt these standards as fundamental principles. At the same time, in addition to the **common human rights**, the **social, economic and cultural human rights** (ref. International Covenant on Economic, Social and Cultural Rights) should be incorporated.

In principle, two approaches are conceivable for the concrete implementation:

The big solution

The core standards of ILO, UNESCO and UNEP will be determined in detail and made universally binding in the context of the WTO. Thus, current sanction mechanisms will be generally applicable, if these standards (in the interpretation agreed upon) are violated.

An intermediate step

If such an extensive consensus cannot be reached, the following is conceivable as an intermediate step: all states involved with the WTO agree to let a subset of states proceed in the direction described - akin to what is discussed on EU level regarding a Europe of two velocities. A scenario where more or less all highly developed countries and only part of the developing countries participate initially is particularly conceivable. For this subset of WTO members, co-financing in return for adherence to standards could be a legitimate rule for international trade transactions within the WTO framework. Funds from co-financing would then only benefit those countries which are willing to accept the preconcerted, maybe development state dependend standards. WTO sanctions in this context would probably be confined to the reduction or cessation of co-financing, if participating (developing) countries infringed the preconcerted standards. Any developing country would be free to join into this solution at any time. Before long, this should **create a pull**. This would provide the basis for the big solution.

IV. What time exposure has to be expected?

The core regulatory framework required for the described processes should be fixable within a few months by persons of appropriate international background. Its length should be manageable. To formulate the linkage of regimes is not the problem. It remains to be seen if there is a **willingness to do so** or, more to the point: if it is possible to find an agreement on **adequate volumes of co-financing**, on how to raise the respective funds, and on implementation procedures. As indicated, the consensus needed on WTO level can take either the form of a big solution, or that of an intermediate step.

Although the central formulation of the global contract will be possible within a document of manageable length, the appendices treating technical subquestions will be longer.

To determine the **financing means** and to codify mechanisms specifying how **the flow of funds will be directed,** and cut off where necessary, will prove substantially more laborious. How is the implementation of standards going to be supported, followed up, and also verified, as the case may be? These are complex questions. A lot of work is required here, and experts will have to invest a substantial amount of consideration.

The same is true for the establishment of a **legal authority of last instance,** which will be necessary. The task of this authority will be to render final judgments in cases of ambiguity as to how the overall solution will affect the individual regimes included. Experts for the individual regimes should be integrated into the respective legal structures, ensuring professional competence and keeping the **new structure required lean**.

Summary

Realizing a viable gobal governance system means to work out a critical element within a complex mosaic. To have correctly identified this issue may be the major intellectual contribution of the Global Marshall Plan Initiative. It has enabled us to state that a "Global Deal" can be accomplished in a manageable timeframe, provided that there is the intention to do so. The idea should be further elaborated by experts. If a respective EU advisory board was established by the end of 2004, the task could be done within 2005/2006. Thus, the Initiative's hope for a start of the Global Marshall Plan by January 1st, 2008 seems feasible at this stage.

The implementation should be kept as **independent as possible of the present international development cooperation.** This Initiative is about **new instruments** of implementation for which new financing volumes are provided. This also implies that the new structures are not intended to undermine the grown structures of development cooperation. Instead, a parallel existence and a close interaction is deemed wise and possible.

V. Total Financial Volume Required

The Zedillo Report estimates that the financial volume required until 2015 will amount to approximately US$ 1 trillion. A schedule for implementation deemed realistic on the part of the Global Marshall Plan Initiative is the period between 2008 and 2015. Taking the additional commitments made until now by certain countries into account, an average of US$ 105 billion in additional funds will be required per year. This is a substantial amount, but it can be accomplished.

The Global Marshall Plan aims at the realization of the UN Millennium Development Goals. On questions of procedure and on funds needed on top of those available for development cooperation today, the United Nations have convened an **international high-level panel on Financing** for Development of major international experts. Under the leadership of the former president of Mexico, Ernesto Zedillo, this panel has produced extensive results in 2001 (the so-called **Zedillo Report** [www.un.org/reports/financing/full_report.pdf]. The UN Zedillo Report contains precise notions on the financing required for a Global Marshall Plan, akin to the views held by the British Chancellor of the Exchequer **Gordon Brown** in his White Paper for the Earth Summit Rio+10 in Johannesburg 2002 [www.globalpolicy.org/socecon/ffd/2002/1216brown.htm], and by **George Soros** in his reflections on establishing **open societies** worldwide [108, 109].

***Gordon Brown**, British Chancellor of the Exchequer*

"Just as the Marshall Plan combined enormous help and a unifying vision to help rebuild Europe after World War II, so must today's rich countries transfer the resources necessary to secure a working economy in all parts of the world that would permit the emergency of political and social conditions in which free institutions can exist."

A **study by the World Bank** dating from 2002 produced similar figures [118]. It estimates that US$ 10 to 15 billion per year are necessary to achieve the Millennium Development Goals with regard to training and education, US$ 20 to 30 billion for health issues, and a further US$ 10 billion for measures concerning water and environment. The report **"Financing Water for all"** [140] by the World Panel on Financing Water Infrastructure from 2003 [www.adb.org/Water/water_financing_wg.asp] claims that in 2000, 1.1 billion people had no safe access to water, and 2.4 billion people were without sufficient means of waste water disposal. To accomplish the Millennium Development Goals pertaining to water on the most basic level, US$ 10 billion per year will be needed until 2015. To achieve a full standard for all people, attainable at best by 2025, more than ten times this sum in additional annual investments would be required in the respective countries, on top of the current US$ 80 billion per year.

These figures are confirmed by a UN report on the status of implementation of the UN Millennium Declaration [128], which takes up on the aforementioned idea of the British Chancellor of the Exchequer Gordon Brown on an **International Finance Facility** (topic 70). Attention should also be paid to a text [26] stating on the basis of an analytical model for the World Bank that new investments by the developing countries of annually 5 5 % GDP will be necessary in this context, namely about US$ 465 billion per year between 2005 and 2010. (This statement refers to the purchasing power-adjusted GDP of these countries, which is higher than the dollar-adjusted GDP. Concerning a GDP calculation based on the dollar, like in this text, this amounts to about 10 % of the GDP of these countries). According to their analysis, the funds should primarily be used for **telecommunications** (US $ 187 billion), **energy** (US $ 138 billion) and roads, including maintenance (US $ 90 billion). The sectoral funds of the financing model listed in chapter VI, table 1 would thus allow to raise about 15 % of the necessary funds through co-financing.

As is the case for the Millennium Development Goals themselves, an extensive international consensus exists on the financial means required, a fact that facilitates the situation for the Global Marshall Plan Initiative at this point. In addition to the funds available for international cooperation at present - approximately US$ 56 billion per year – the Zedillo Report states that another **US$ 50 billion** for **general investments** in achieving the Millennium Development Goals, and **US$ 20 billion** for a **worldwide provision of public goods** for the benefit and security of all human beings will be needed per year until 2015. **UNICEF** also estimates the volume of funds required for the worldwide provision of **basic social services**, corresponding to a progressive compliance with economic, social and cultural human rights, to amount to additional funds of approximately US$ 70 billion per year. In the context of the Millennium Development Goals, public goods refer specifically to such topics as [55]:

- Realization of fundamental human rights for all, including universal access to basic education and health systems
- Respect of national sovereignty
- Worldwide preventive health care, in particular the fight against transmittable diseases
- Worldwide security, or in other words, a global public area void of crime and violence
- World Peace
- Transfrontier harmonization of communication and transport systems
- Transfrontier harmonization of institutional infrastructures, in support of goals like market efficiency, universal human rights, transparent and accountable government, or harmonization of technical standards
- Concerted knowledge management, including global respect for intellectual property rights
- Concerted management of global natural common goods, in support of their sustainable utilization
- Availability of secure international locations for multilateral negotiations, both between states and between governmental and non-governmental actors

Considering the total sum required between 2002 and 2015, an additional **US$ 980 billion** have to be raised. UN reports on the status of funds for the Millennium Development Goals state that an additional annual sum of US$ 12 billion will be available from 2006 onwards, due to commitments undertaken by certain developed countries in the meantime. This amounts to US$ 120 billion in new funds; **US$ 860 billion** are still lacking. The proposal developed in this text aims for these funds to be raised between 2008 and 2015. It must be pointed out in this context that in the final stage from 2011 until 2015, this is a matter of an annual co-financing volume of approximately US$ 180 billion, including the funds presently employed for development cooperation. This amounts to about 0.6 % of the **world gross domestic** product. Then, finally, the world would have reached the long-aspired stage where the developed countries invest about 0.7 % of their GDP in development cooperation. To achieve long-term **eradication of poverty** and **sustainability** on this globe, more funds will likely be needed, and for a longer period of time after 2015. But with a Global Marshall Plan, the all-important step of entrance into a sustainable design would finally have been accomplished.

The funds to be raised by the world community under the terms of a Global Marshall Plan must be employed in a targeted, transparent and **accountable** manner for the goals collectively aimed at, as has already been discussed in this text. The **intellectual design** and **management** of the actual processes present a great challenge. This is why a **sufficiently long process for design and verification** until 2007 is deemed necessary. Implementation could then begin from January 1st, 2008. A step-by-step plan for a chronological implementation, taking up on considerations in [87], will be presented below. With regard to the **Rio+15 World Summit** dated at that stage, the governmental heads of the world could promote the adoption of this plan as a contribution to a sustainable development.

A proposal for a schedule for implementation of the Global Marshall Plan

Fall 2004

A campaign for the convention of an EU advisory board for the elaboration of a Global Marshall Plan is launched, targeting the EU Parliament, the EU Commission and the EU Council, the national parliaments of EU member states and selected international organizations. Its tasks would include **objectives, required funds, implementation mechanisms, measures, schedule, partners and actors**.

The convention of such an Advisory Board is the short-term goal of the Initiative **Global Marshall Plan / Planetary Contract**. Simultaneously, approval on the part of the business and the NGOs shall be sought. The activities targeting the EU Parliament and the EU Commission are scheduled for the EU Parliament elections in summer 2004, and the restructuring of the EU commission due later in this summer.

Fall/Winter 2004

The EU convenes an Advisory Board on the topic, which produces a report. The text at hand and other contributions can serve as input for this task.

Summer/Fall 2005

The proposal of a Global Marshall Plan / Planetary Contract becomes (hopefully) the EU's official position for all future World Summits.

2006

A worldwide consensus on a Planetary Contract is achieved (as regards partners, schedule, financial volume, fund raising, linking to standards, institutional design, implementation mechanisms, compliance and controlling). This also includes ideas on how respective measures will be carried on beyond 2015.

2007
Preparations for the implementation of the consensus reached are on the way in all participating international organizations and actors, as is the **adjustment of all implicated international agreements.** A legal authority of **last instance** is established by linking elements of various existing international legal and compliance structures, particularly those of the WTO.

2007
Within an appropriate context of **Rio+15**, the implementation of the Global Marshall Plan / Planetary Contract is finalized.

2008–2015
Implementation phase.

VI. Raising and Utilization of Funds – Issues of Central Importance

Institutions already exist that can administrate the transactions necessary for implementing a Global Marshall Plan. It must however be clear that the respective support programs **must not repeat the mistakes of past decades of development**. This applies to the donor countries (large-scale projects, excessive red tape etc.), but particularly to the receiving countries (corrupt potentates, capital flight, the suppression of a socio-economic development which would allow for the formation of a middle class, and a lacking disposition to cooperate regionally). Key to gaining acceptance for a Global Marshall Plan are clear statements on improved support programs and practices, both concerning the manifold experiences and corresponding **further opening of markets** by the rich countries.

New, innovative approaches are required for the raising and employment of funds in the context of a Global Marshall Plan, i.e. for both financing and implementation. This is because development assistance programs in the past often fell short of their potential success. For example, disproportionate enrichment of local elites, or as a priority target, the **employment of experts or companies from the donor countries** occurred time and again, as did support for projects which were not sustainable beyond the cessation of foreign aid. In this context, the **fight against corruption** linked to an agreement on standards plays a vital role, and should **involve discerning NGOs** like **Transparency International** (www.transparency.org) [122], whose contribution for **facilitating better conditions for development** is extremely important. With regard to the new funds to be raised, efficient implementation mechanisms are crucial to gain wide-spread support for the proposal of a Global Marshall Plan / Planetary Contract. Respective measures and programs would have to be designed by an **(international) advisory board convened by the EU**. This has already been discussed in chapter II.

Depending on how the funds are raised, linking with the fund-raising organization named in the succeeding proposal would be reasonable, e.g. IMF or WTO. This would entail repercussions for the future architecture of financial markets and international trade [14, 59, 87, 109, 110, 111]. Programmatically, funds from a potential tax on world trade could be partly allocated to those **economic sectors** they stem from, and which are **particularly relevant for development objectives**, e.g. telecommunications or energy. Thus, the **raising and allocation of funds is transparently interlinked**, a plausible method which is likely to significantly increase approval of concerned actors. Under the terms of this proposal, proceeds would primarily accrue at IMF and WTO. In terms of the standards implemented and the respective procedures, the WB, ILO, UNEP, UNDP, UNESCO, UNFPA and others would also be implicated. Therefore, these partner organizations have to be substantially involved in the formulation and implementation of the respective programs.

In the following, a **proposal** will be presented as a model for further discussion, exemplifying how the required volumes can be raised and allocated, easily modifiable. To link fundraising to **adequate opening of markets** by the developed countries remains a vital element for a Global Marshall Plan. **Direct governmental payments** to an international coordinating entity like the World Bank, as practiced in the EU depending on the gross domestic product of the respective country, e.g., will not be aimed for to avoid acceptance problems. Similar effects can be achieved by using **Special Drawing Rights of the IMF**, a proposal initiated by **George Soros** [109]. Also for acceptance reasons, special taxes on **socially encumbering activities** (e.g. in the military sector) will not be discussed here; nor will specific charges for **disproportionate utilization of resources, or the induction of extensive environmental degradation**, except when respective world trade activities are implicated in a Terra tax on international trade. These exclusions are due to purely pragmatic reasons, and are but a suggestion. As mentioned above, there are other approaches with high potential, e.g. the establishment of a Future Fund as **Maximilian Gege** proposes, or the **International Finance Facility** brought forward by British Chancellor of the Exchequer **Gordon Brown**. **H. W. Zillmer** of the "Foundation Children in Africa" suggests the establishment of a **"Global Development Fund"** based on a global CO_2 tax. If it was paid by all countries at a rate of US$ 5 per ton CO_2 emissions, such a tax would raise more than US$ 100 billion per year without affecting competitiveness, charging all countries corresponding to their respective stage of industrialization (using the CO_2-emission per country as levelling rule) [147].

Against this background, the author's proposal should be seen as an example offering manifold options for modification. Any other form of funding would be equally welcome, as long as it supports the aspired goals, particularly the **implementation of the United Nations Development Goals** until 2015.

Millennium Development Compact [126]

International financial institutions should put the Millennium Development Goals at the centre of their analytical, advisory and financing efforts for every developing country.

1. Fundraising at the International Monetary Fund (IMF)

One of the particularly interesting approaches on raising funds was initiated by **George Soros**, whose book "George Soros on Globalization" [109] offers essential insight into global economical problems by a renowned adept of international financial markets. This approach uses the so-called **Special Drawing Rights** [50]. A country will be granted funds depending on the quota it has paid into the IMF Fund, to use under the terms of the international financial architecture, similar to currency reserves. The "trick" is that developing countries pay part of their quota in their own often comparatively weak currency, while being disbursed in strong currencies from the Special Drawing Rights' currency basket. George Soros believes such a utilization of **Special Drawing Rights** at the IMF, namely as **Matching Funds for Social Entrepreneurship**, to be the essential approach towards a better organization of worldwide development.

Special drawing rights can in fact be regarded as a (hidden) part of a **direct new generation of money** and loaning it, an instrument commonly used on the national level by the (central) banks of issue **for the financial "mirroring" of economic growth, similar to effectuating inflation by generating and loaning new money**. The same applies to money generation in the private banking sector, which is bound to interest payments to the governments and is reflected in revenue of central banks, for example. In Germany, this revenue amounted to Euro 11.2 billion in 2001, and 5.4 billion in 2002.

The proposal to use Special Drawing Rights for the support of international development is also taken up in the **Zedillo Report** (www.un.org/reports/financing/full_report.pdf) and by the British Chancellor of the Exchequer **Gordon Brown**, both in his White Paper on the topic [www.globalpolicy.org/socecon/ffd/2002/1216brown.htm] and in the document partly quoted above [13]. In the scale discussed here, this proposal would noticeably reduce the respective national options of the developed countries, because of its redistribution effect in favor of the developing countries. Good will assumed, it should still be possible.

Special Drawing Rights are an established instrument of the IMF (www.imf.org) and have been used in the past. An additional (singular) volume of US$ **27.5 billion** is **in preparation** at the IMF and has already gained 75% of the votes, but is still lacking the US congress' approval to obtain the required quota of at least 85% of votes. In this issue the US have a power of veto.

Concerning the proposal currently submitted to the IMF [109], **George Soros** suggests that **this level of Special Drawing Rights** should be generated annually in the future. Under their own agenda, the rich countries should allocate their stake of US$ 18 billion to co-financing programs for development cooperation, subject to certain conditions. These funds could thus be seen as development assistance or direct governmental transfer payments. As has been stressed before, **demographic policy measures regarding reproductive health** are of vital importance for a better future and therefore should play a major part in this context. To this end, dedicated states should mobilize an additional US$ 3 to 4 billion per year as co-financing contribution for implementing the resolutions of the World Summit in Cairo 1994. **In the context of a Global Marshall Plan, this is a manageable sum**.

Under the terms of the IMF, the poorer countries' Special Drawing Rights are significantly lower, due to the small dimension of their own quotas (about a third of the total volume), but would additionally and directly benefit these countries, e.g. by **enhancing their currency reserves**. George Soros [109] also provides many details for a reasonable utilization of these funds, avoiding earlier mistakes; some of these will be discussed below. The proposal made in the text at hand slightly extends George Soros' approach by opting for annual expenditures of US$ 30 - 40 billion in IMF special drawing rights for North-South transfers during the period of 2008 to 2015. If the quota of the developing countries, amounting to about one third of the total volume, was used as additional benefit instead of a contribution to co-financing measures, the total volume of such Drawing Rights would have to be increased to US$ 45 - 60 billion.

To generate the required revenues, a so-called **Tobin tax** on financial transactions is also considered promising within the international debate (refer to [24] and information provided by the Tobin Tax Initiative [120]). **Maartje van Putten** [80] remarks on this:

***Maartje van Putten** [80]*

> "That actions are focused on global financial transactions and capital flows makes sense. According to The Economist, the situation is as follows, '...twenty years ago there was very little cross-border trade in bonds or shares. It now accounts for about $ 600 billion in bonds every day and $ 30 billion in equities [The Economist, 23 Oct 1999].
>
> Derivative trading amounted to about $ 30 trillion a year in 1994 and $ 120 trillion in 2001 or four times global GDP [The Economist, 7 Oct 1995, 18 May 2002]."

The proposal at hand takes up on the idea of a Tobin tax, although many argue against it. Most of the counter-arguments find fault in the **restriction of speculation on the currency markets** which is indeed wanted by many in favor of a Tobin tax, or state that to go it alone on a national or European level would be counterproductive for Europe [8, 138]. In our context, however, these arguments are not substantial, as our (primary) **aim is not the restriction of speculation, and our scope is a global one**. Provided that the rich countries come to a respective agreement, uncooperative countries can be forced into participating in a Tobin tax by purely fiscal means. Nor will this tax discriminate international cooperation; on the contrary, global finance transactions provide an attractive **new** dimension of value-adding on which taxes can be imposed accordingly.

A Tobin tax is one of the major requests raised by the globalization designers from the **alliance ATTAC** [31, 32, 38]. Persons and groups active within ATTAC are often defamed by the media as **anti-globalization activists**, against their better judgment (a success of the so-called **Public Awareness Management**), despite the fact that the declared goal of

Attac is to organize a globalization that has got out of hand to the advantage of most people. The **organization of globalization** is also a motivation of the Global Marshall Plan Initiative and a central demand raised by the ILO World Commission in their report on the **social dimension of globalization** cited above. George Soros arguments along the same lines.

The Tobin tax is being endorsed more and more as a form of financing. On July 1st 2004 the Belgium parliament decided to support the implementation of a Tobin tax. The law is well designed insofar as it binds implementation to the support of such a tax all over Europe. Concerning the volumes, the proposal goes for a 0.02 per cent amount, as also proposed in this text. The Belgium decision follows support by France, which passed the law in 2001. The growing support in Europe is encouraging. However, eventually a worldwide solution is required.

Again: the objective of a Tobin tax as it is presented here is not what the economist James Tobin (www.ceedweb.org/iirp) aimed for primarily, i.e. restricting speculative transactions; this intention is barely a background motive here. Instead, the objective is to generate investment funds for a worldwide development from those globalization processes which asymetrically benefit comparatively few actors, both through **new creation of money** (by banks of issue) and **access to credits**, as well as through **global financial markets**. Nor shall this money be spent in the form of classical development cooperation by governments, but according to new, innovative, and particularly **investment orientated mechanisms**, as has already been discussed in this text. All this aims at a **world economic miracle**, and is supposed to make the world richer.

However, the topic requires further analysis. In part due to textual issues, but mainly because of the **massive problem of acceptance** pertaining to this topic. A tender spot **in the prevalent structures of power, property and access** is touched, a "Holy Grail" particularly for all market fundamentalist doctrines. This area is **taboo** and tends to be almost reflexively defended with a bulwark.

The dimension dealt with in the following requires some clarification. While the world gross domestic product currently amounts to approximately US$ 30 trillion and world trade to 8.5 trillion annually, **international finance transactions** amount to **US$ 480 trillion a year**. Thus, a tax rate of merely 0.01% would generate funds of US$ 30 billion per year, even if the trade volume on financial markets should lapse from the current US$ 480,000 trillion to US$ 300,000 trillion as a consequence of this new tax.

There is massive resistance against a Tobin tax. Basically because the willingness is lacking to raise these funds for international development, particularly by charging those who benefit most from the globalization of the financial markets and the new value-adding potential they offer. Yet the argument brought forward most often is that the **collective intelligence of the global financial markets** would be threatened. This has been thoroughly and visibly refuted, at the latest since the most recent scandals on the financial markets, and the breakdown of Financial Bubbles like the New Economy. **George Soros** in his exceedingly clear books on the topic fittingly judges the errors in reasoning and the misconceptions by those market fundamentalists who still choose to believe in collective intelligence and stability in the face of obvious **speculation on instability** [107, 109]. Years before the actual fact, the author predicted the unavoidable collapse of the New Economy and its scale, though not the time of occurrence. The whole structure resembled a Ponzi scheme, or a chain letter situation [85].

Another frequently used but equally inadequate argument states that such a tax would interfere with global value-adding. Banks and brokers already impose fees on international financial transactions. And if charges on value-adding processes were a fundamental problem, why is it done on the national level? Finally, all arguments denouncing too high administrative expenses are only partially applicable, because **worldwide transborder financial transactions** are already fully electronic. Thus, recording and debiting a Tobin tax would easily be possible, and the administrative and bureaucratic overhead small. However, as part of the formal accounts **only apply to daily balances**, a major part of the chargeable volume would remain unrecorded. This aspect requires further analysis.

Funds raised by these means could be allocated directly to the IMF, in interaction with the World Bank, or invested in the context of development programs. Within the framework of a Global Marshall Plan, all future loans granted within a "Global Deal" in the form aspired here would be subject to adherence to core standards of the ILO, UNESCO and UNEP; a substantial change from current policies regulated by the Washington Consensus. Additionally, the IMF could utilize these funds to mitigate **currency crises** better than today, and together with the World Bank and other partners, to help initiating development programs in afflicted or highly indebted countries, in return for the willingness of these countries to implement certain standards wherever feasible. The **Comprehensive Poverty Reduction Process** of IMF and World Bank also prepares **further debt relief for the poorest countries** under certain conditions. A crucial part plays the HIPC Initiative for the heavily indebted poor countries.

Of equal importance and under discussion for years is the establishment of **regulated bankruptcy proceedings for states**, and part of the respective funding. In the case of an economic collapse, the private sector could then be involved as a donor with the solution of a problem often enough caused by its support of deficient programs, making the over-indebtedness possible in the first place. Furthermore, the IMF could provide means to the World Bank, at its disposal within the so-called **"Comprehensive Development Framework"**. This would substantially increase the World Bank's scope of means, currently amounting to about US$ 100 million per year gained from interests.

In this context, George Soros mentions the **International Development Association** (IDA) created in 1960 by the World Bank to grant the poorest countries low-interest loans, the **International Finance Cooperation** (IFC) which provides investments and credits to the private sector, and the **Multilateral Investment Guarantee Agency** (MIGA) which plays an important role for the Poverty Reduction Strategy of IMF and World Bank.

George Soros indicates that the World Bank's support of development has changed towards an integrated approach, partly **following a new, less market fundamentalist logic** [109]. That is a good thing. However, the World Bank can spend only comparatively little of its scarce **free funds for co-financing** on these reasonable new approaches. A decisive step in this direction is long overdue, and could be funded through a Global Marshall Plan. The **financially solid institutions of IMF and World Bank** and the international controls pertaining to them provide the preconditions for allocating new funds in a different, more targeted, more effective and **more accountable way** than today. And in time, this will possibly have a formative bearing on an even better utilization of the current funds for development cooperation.

To round off the remarks made in chapter II [109] provides further interesting clues on this topic, aiming at co-financing local projects **competing for support**. Co-financing large private funds facing the worldwide challenges is also taken into consideration, as well as the involvement of regional institutions (in analogy to **EU Structural Funds** procedures), or a massive involvement of NGOs. Finally, it is of vital importance that the major part of the money - i.e. substantially more than at present - **must reach the local people** facing the problems, instead of financing experts and companies from the donor countries, even if their involvement will always be necessary to a certain degree where their specific expertise is required to solve a problem. This demand has been repeatedly and convincingly pronounced and justified by **George Soros** [108, 109] as well as by **Muhammad Yunus,** founder of the Grameenbank and a major **mentor of the micro credit movement**, [145], and other scientists studying the economy of poverty like **Hernando de Soto** [17] and **Amartya Sen** [104].

2. Fund raising within the World Trade Organization

The WTO is a **particularly important international organization** and provides the decisive institutional foundation for world economy today. The WTO's jurisdiction and **massive sanctioning options through the approval of penal duties** deserve special mention here. In contrast to IMF and World Bank, the WTO is significantly more **"democratic"** with regard to the poorer countries' potential to exert influence, because it is based on the **principle of consensus**. Even so, the richer countries can enforce unfair solutions within WTO consensus, by utilizing their **advantages as regards knowledge and organization**, and their potential to punctually apply their **larger economical power** (e.g. by offering local concessions). The recent failure of the **development round in Cancun** proved that the poorer world could nonetheless block further agreements. The blockade of Cancun has to be overcome. An important topic in this regard is the **further opening of markets** by the rich countries for the benefit of the developing, primarily the poorest countries. Experts worldwide agree that **stopping all agricultural export subsidies by the rich countries** is long overdue.

George Soros is generally right in saying that **if it did not already exist, the WTO would have to be invented** [109]. However, the future problem is to enforce not only trade issues, but also those pertaining to global social and ecological concerns. To this end, the **WTO, as well as IMF and World Bank, should be institutionally linked to other regulatory bodies in an intelligent way** [87, 109]. An adequate coupling of all respective international regimes as described above is the main objective of a Planetary Contract. This is why the WTO is of highest institutional importance for the proposal made in this text. The WTO is to be **the core of a global governance system which ensures sustainability**, by which core elements of ILO, UNESCO, and global environmental standards will be made binding for world trade and loans granted for development projects, possibly together with IMF and World Bank, and with the approval of all partners (gained with co-financing offers on part of the developed world).

This would be the **first step towards a worldwide Eco-Social Market Economy** [87, chapter 28], a **Balanced Way**. As demanded on the World Summit in Rio 1992, trade and development must be interconnected, accompanied by high protective standards. Because of the WTO's consensus principle, **win-win solutions** have the best prospects of implementation in the long run.

However, the WTO offers a second starting point for supporting the development of solutions. Besides global financial transactions, international trade with its special potentials for adding value could directly contribute to the funding of worldwide development. To this end, agreements on a tax on global trade (**Terra tax**) should be found within the WTO [21, 87, 96, 110, 111], to be used to **fund investments in development**. This corresponds to the basic idea of the so-called Fair Trade, propagated and organized by NGOs and churches, among others. Suitable solutions have been established for certain import goods of poorer countries like, e.g., **carpets** and **coffee**, albeit only partly and on a voluntary basis. The proposed **Terra (investment) tax** should extend the scope to world trade in total, and render the principle universally binding. Funds generated by a Terra tax should mainly be employed as **investments** supporting development concerns, but also for achieving a better balance between cultures, and for environmental protection - thus, for achieving **sustainability aims** at large. This concept is fully compatible with the UN Millennium Development Goals, **makes the world a richer place overall**, and will be substantiated in the following. It is important to note that this approach **makes particular sense to private enterprise**. Many companies and first trade associations have already expressed respective ideas. Especially popular in this context is the selective utilization of such funds for investment programs targeting crucial infrastructure areas, e.g. energy and telecommunications.

As has been stated above, **international trade** currently amounts to an estimated annual volume of about US$ 8.5 trillion including US$ 6.3 trillion in real assets, US$ 1.6 trillion in internationally traded services, and US$ 0.9 trillion in information and communication services. The latter are yet to be associated with the WTO.

States keep detailed **trade registers** because of custom duties and, partly, value-added taxes due at the borders. By using the **administrative structures pertaining to customs or financial management**, the raising of a minor surcharge on international trade with goods could be realized without major administrative effort. This surcharge could then be made directly available for projects, e.g. through the WTO. A tax rate of 0.5 % on world trade would currently raise about US$ 44 billion annually for the support of worldwide development. Such a 0.5% surcharge is barely noticeable, considering that for most products, import costs are well below 50 %

of domestic sales prizes, in most cases even below 20 %, e.g. for bananas, coffee or petrol. The citizens are used to very different dimensions, i.e. with regard to fluctuations of the Dollar price for crude oil, the additional fluctuations caused by exchange rate changes, and finally the frequent tax increases on petrol. According to the German Federal Statistical Office, prices for mineral oil products increased by 4.4 % in Germany in 2003. This is about **50 times the value of the proposed Terra tax**, as this increase relates to the final price and not the import price for crude oil. The Terra tax would amount to about US$ 1 per one ton of crude oil. Such a contribution for international development has long been demanded by the president of the Club of Rome, **HRH Prince El Hassan bin Talal** [23].

On the part of the WTO, funds could be allocated directly and exclusively to those developing countries which as WTO members actually **implement** concerted core elements of the **ILO or environmental standards**. Simultaneously, the WTO could use the services of the World Bank for implementation tasks, e.g. for programs designed to **overcome illiteracy**, etc.. The same applies to the **bridging of the digital divide and establishing telecommunication infrastructures**. In this case, the International Communication Union (ITU) would be an adequate partner.

The allocation of funds to special market segments, e.g. for funding **investment programs for infrastructure in developing countries,** is of special interest in this context. For example, by imposing a Terra tax rate of 0.5 % on international telecommunications transactions, US$ 4.5 billion could be raised for respective measures, e.g. the **Digital Solidarity Fund**, demanded, as yet unsuccessfully, by the developing world at the World Summit for an Information Society (WSIS) in Geneva December 2003.

With the Terra tax quota on energy source transfers, the construction of **worldwide energy systems** could be funded, particularly with regard to **alternative energies** [71, 121]. A tax rate of 0.5 % would yield about US$ 3.1 billion in respective funds. In this context, a possible role for the OPEC has to be further considered.

Concerning **agriculture**, approximately US$ 2.9 billion are urgently needed for an expansion in the South of the globe (the current volume of development assistance in this area amounts to about US$ 8 billion a year). This has to be accompanied by a clear **prohibition of all export subsidies on agricultural products** going from the rich to the developing countries, and by concerted further opening of agricultural markets in the North. However, **multifunctional aspects** of the role of agriculture have to be taken into account as proposed by the EU; for an elaboration on this point, please refer to [87, 142]. In some parts, the EU export subsidies have accumulated to 40 % of the EU's budget for agriculture, which itself amounts to 0.4 to 0.5 % of the EU gross domestic product. Thus we are talking about up to 0.2 % of the EU gross domestic product. This is more than half the cumulative development assistance of all EU member states.

It has to be pointed out that **pure free trade is not the right approach to deal with the hardships pertaining to global food issues** [87, 142]. Instead, the social, cultural and ecological standards would have to be globally harmonized and co-financed to begin with, as aspired by an eco-social Global Marshall Plan. Only subject to those conditions will prizes, e.g. **transportation prizes, tell the truth** in the long run. Consequently, the exchange relations between North and South will change, in this case in favour of the agriculture in the North, particularly where goods of low added value are concerned.

Better than free trade is a co-financed system of mutual support and positive interaction in consideration of **multifunctionality requirements**. If the rich countries decline this, **free trade will become the legitimate request of the poor**, which is better than nothing and pedals the rich in terms of justification. For there is an obvious **credibility gap** when it comes to the rich world, namely in the **"dishonesty" of an argumentation** selectively targeting unregulated free trade where this is to its own advantage, while refusing to abstain from protecting its own fields of added value, whenever the developing world turns out to be more competitive.

In any case, the international verdict is that pure free trade would worsen the situation of the poorer countries' agricultural sector and in particular the situation of peasants, whose economic, social and cultural human rights would be undermined. This is also true for fisheries (industrial fishery of rich countries competing with traditional local fisheries), as well as for many **large-scale projects supported by developed** countries or international organizations (e.g. through loans or securities), for example the **building of dams or mining projects**. In many cases, internationally active corporations from the donor countries are substantially involved in these projects.

As mentioned, this has led to a debate within science [97] and NGOs in Germany [139] on the question whether supporting such projects can be reconciled at all with the commitments made by the German Federal Government, e.g. when joining the **International Covenant on Economic, Social and Cultural Rights** (ICESCR) in 1996. This pact implies a direct duty of the rich countries to help wherever people's rights are directly threatened, even though the scope of this duty is not determined. What this pact entails at any rate, however, is the duty to **refrain from any action that would worsen the situation of the most afflicted**. Yet in the fields mentioned, the contrary is often the case. It has already been mentioned that the World Bank now addresses this issue [119]. At the latest, the framework of a Planetary Contract should guarantee that if such projects are supported in the future, at least adequate compensations for the people concerned must be ensured, e.g. in the fishing sector. With regard to agricultural exports, the above mentioned **complete cessation of any kind of export subsidies by rich countries must be the minimal target**.

Concerning **pharmaceutical products** (generating US$ 500 million per year), the objective is to utilize the international health sector funds for the development and short-term disposal of new pharmaceutical products (while allowing for a certain reward for intellectual property rights). In this context, the achievements of the **Gates Foundation** with an annual budget of US$ 1 billion should be mentioned; these activities could be supported further.
The annual global **military expenses** were estimated to amount to about US$ 794 billion in 2002 - **a disaster, given the social misery on this globe**. The increase from the previous year was 6 %, i.e. with about US$ 48 billion nearly as high as the total global development aid. This increase took place mainly in the US. The trend continued in 2003. According to official figures, the export of weapons amounted to (only) US$ 35 billion. There is no doubt that by establishing a more peaceful and balanced world, **military expenses should be massively reduced** in the medium term. In the meantime, compensation measures should be introduced at the very least . A Terra tax of 0.35 % or 0.5 % levied on the trade flows of all weapons legally traded internationally would raise funds of about US$ 120 million or 180 million, respectively. This money could be employed globally for reconstruction, support of war orphans and victims of mines, clearing of minefields, and **peace research**. Given the moral issues implied with military goods, a higher Terra quota on these would stand to reason; but for reasons of practicality, this line of thought will not be further pursued here.

Finally, the future design of the **contract of Kyoto** could provide another interesting source of funds for development from 2012, by a fair (equal amount per capita) assignment of pollution rights and their trading worldwide [72, 87, 136, 137]. This topic will be elaborated subsequently. Presently, **the North is "stealing" pollution rights** without paying a compensation, which the South will urgently need at some stage for its future development. If the **North would finally pay for what it continuously appropriates without financial compensation at the expense of the South**, this alone would cover a considerable part of the funds needed for a Planetary Contract (an estimated minimum of US$ 40 billion per year).

Until such reasoning becomes practicable, the promising **CDM mechanism** of the Kyoto Protocol could already be utilized on short notice in terms of an **worldwide Eco-Social Market Economy**. Unfortunately, this is very rarely the case, but would be possible anytime according to current contracts [87]. In addition to this, the Terra tax could be used to finally adequately fund the UN's **Global Environmental Facility** for financing projects for CO_2 reduction in the South. Of course, funds that may be raised in the future context of a fair trade with CO_2 emission rights could also be used as an additional **source of funds** for worldwide development beyond the year 2015. The text at hand is in favor of this option.

According to the study [148], global **CO_2 emissions** from fossil fuels currently amount to about 25 billion tons per year. Of these, 14.5 billion tons are generated by the North (in this context: the Annex B states of the Kyoto Protocol) with about 20 % of the global population, and 10.5 billion tons by the rest of the states. If the (intermediate) target of reducing total emissions to the status of 1990, i.e. about 22 billion tons, is implemented, and assuming equal emission rights per capita, the Annex B states would be entitled to primary emission rights of about 4.5 billion tons, and thus would have to buy the additional ten billion per year from other states. Incidentally, China by now uses about 75 % of its share, namely 3.4 billion tons, while India with 1.05 billion tons is still at about 29%.I

For the time being, **reforestation programs** and other measures for generating new CO_2 sinks could be realized, and various solutions using **solar energy** could substantially save CO_2 emissions in countries receiving a high amount of sunshine. Currently, such approaches calculate about US$ 4 per ton saved, a price that can surely be further reduced under market pressure. On the other hand, the reduction potentials available at low cost are limited, and volume pressure will further increase, causing prices to rise again.

For the moment, let us adopt a price of US$ 4 per ton saved and assume that the North acquires the total amount of additional rights under the terms of a **fair, equal access per capita logic** [87], as also discussed in a **global climate certificate system based on market and incentive mechanisms** [136, 137]. This would raise annually (at least) US$ 40 billion in payments by the North for the benefit of the South, which could be invested in development. Obviously the situation would become more challenging and the costs incurred substantially higher if worldwide CO_2 emissions were to be reduced even further as is discussed internationally, e.g. to 50% of the level of 1990 (eleven billion tons).

Conclusingly, it must be stated that the measures proposed here would require a **substantial increase in staff** at the WTO – long overdue – and significantly more cooperation of it with ILO and particularly with UNEP, as well as other international organizations concerned. This cooperation is already under way but must be increased, especially with regard to the **jurisdiction of last resort** needed within the evolving Global Governance System. The judicial and **sanction options of the WTO** should provide the anchor for this.

VII. Scope of Funds 2008 to 2015

The funds required for a Global Marshall Plan can be clearly itemized, and they are attainable. Strains are minimal and, above all, have to be regarded in due proportion to the achievable benefits - less as costs than as investments generating proceeds.

In addition to many other projected measures, the **Zedillo Report** proposes that on top of the current US$ 56 billion per year, 14 x 70 = US$ 980 billion should be raised within the period 2002 to 2015 for international development. As mentioned, this view is shared by the British Chancellor of the Exchequer **Gordon Brown** in his White Paper for the Rio+10 conference in 2003, and by **George Soros** in his report on globalization [109]. Studies conducted by advisory boards of various UN suborganizations come to similar conclusions. The concept at hand hopes for a process of international consensus with the necessary resolutions ready to be passed by 2007, within the timeframe of **Rio+15**.

Implementation then takes place between 2008 and 2015, also preparing for further efforts after 2015. The **framework of implementation for these new funds should be entirely new**, replacing the instruments mainly used within current development cooperation; a measure which is also likely to increase acceptance on the part of the donors.

The annual sums to be raised for an implementation phase beginning in 2008 exceed those that would have been required if activities had started in 2000. To allow for an optimal utilization of the funds and a gradual adjustment of structures, implementation should occur in two phases: from 2008 to 2011, and from 2012 to 2015. Promising approaches like direct governmental transfers, taxes on economic activities impairing the common good, a fair trade on access to resources and pollution rights, issuance of funds for future-oriented investments, realization of an International Finance Facility, etc. are not discussed here for reasons of practicality. Instead, **three elements** are exemplarily pursued in this proposal:

- transferred **Special Drawing Rights at the IMF** (US$ 30 billion between 2008 and 2011, US$ 40 billion between 2012 and 2015),

- a **Tobin tax** (of 0.01 % in 2008 to 2011, with an annual volume of about US$ 30 billion, and of 0.02 % in 2012 to 2015, with an annual volume of about US$ 40 billion), and finally

- a **Terra tax** (of 0.35 % in 2008 to 2012, with an annual volume of about US$ 30 billion, and 0.5 % in 2012 to 2015, with an annual volume of about US$ 42 billion).

The respective figures are presented below. New commitments to the UN by certain states amounting to US$ 12 billion from 2006 have been taken into account, resulting in US$ 860 billion still to be raised until 2015. The level of international co-financing which will have been reached between 2012 and 2015 will provide a good starting point for the transition into a **worldwide Eco-Social Market Economy**, to be targeted for 2015. By then, **at least 0.7 % of the gross domestic product of donor countries should be ensured for development cooperation**.

Remarks

1.) The sectoral proceeds, namely **investment potentials**, could be implemented directly, e.g. for bridging the **digital divide** or for supporting cooperation concerning food; an option which should be used.

2.) The figures do not include projections concerning future global economic growth and its distribution, to keep things simple and because the general picture would not be affected.

It has to be noted that the total volume of co-financing will amount to more than US$ 190 billion in 2015, compared to US$ 56 billion today. This sum corresponds to the **aspired 0.7 % of the gross national product of the donor countries**, yet represents only about half of what the author believes necessary for a positive worldwide development from 2015 onwards.

However, some experts maintain that substantially less could suffice if the funds were properly used, e.g. in a way similar to a **core element of effective EU integration funds**. These **funds for structural support** are in the scope of 0.27 % of the EU gross domestic product [53].

These suggestions are based on the **support of international investments** subject to social concerns, and on **retransfers from international work-related migration remittances** under an improved design. All these possibilities are regarded as a welcome addition here, as the dimension of the task to be tackled is immense and requires contributions from many parts.

For a correct evaluation of the scope of these funds, which is ultimately based on the UN Zedillo Report [www.un.org/reports/financing/full_report.pdf], it has to be noted that it would **still not suffice to raise the income of the 1 billion poorest people from currently about US$ 0.5 above the threshold of US$ 1 per day** by direct payments in the form of global social welfare. When comparing the worldwide situation with the scope of socially motivated transfers developed countries regard as **necessary to establish balance and ensure a perspective for all** within their own borders, the exertions ahead become obvious. If a mere US$ 1 of social welfare a day were to be handed to the poorer half of mankind - the minimum transfer volume under the terms of a world democracy - **US$ 1,000 billion** a year would have to be raised. This calculation reveals yet again the immense discrepancies prevalent on this globe today.

However, direct transfers do not come to the fore in the proposal for a Global Marshall Plan. Such transfers are not efficient enough, although they may become additionally necessary to save the poorest from hunger and hardship. Our main focus is on **"Seed Money"**, i.e. indirect effects exerting a **large leverage effect**, as can be observed with the current EU warranties for micro credit banks providing the latter with AAA refinancing options on financial markets. Large leverage effects are at the core of this proposal, allowing for a multiple of effects through **indirectly induced growth** than would be possible through direct transfers.

Terra Tax (sectoral) in billion US$

	2006	2007	2008	2009	2010	2011	2012	2013	2014	2015	
Telecommunications (US$ 900 billion)	0	0	3.15	3.15	3.15	3.15	4.5	4.5	4.5	4.5	**30.60**
Energy (US$ 620 billion)	0	0	2.17	2.17	2.17	2.17	3.1	3.1	3.1	3.1	**21.08**
Agriculture (US$ 580 billion)	0	0	2.03	2.03	2.03	2.03	2.9	2.9	2,9	2.9	**19.72**
Pharmaceutical products (US$ 100 billion)	0	0	0.35	0.35	0.35	0.35	0.5	0.5	0.5	0.5	**3.40**
Military expenses (US$ 35 billion)	0	0	0.12	0.12	0.12	0.12	0.18	0.18	0.18	0.18	**1.19**

Additional sources for the funding of the Millennium Goals in billion US$												
	2002-2005	**2006**	**2007**	**2008**	**2009**	**2010**	**2011**	**2012**	**2013**	**2014**	**2015**	
Development aid today	224	56	56	56	56	56	56	56	56	56	56	
Additional commitments (from 2006)	0	12	12	12	12	12	12	12	12	12	12	**120**
Special Drawing Rights (supported by the North; benefiting developing countries)	0	0	0	30	30	30	30	40	40	40	40	**280**
Tobin Tax (imposed on US$ 300 / 200 trillion): 0.01 % 2008 to 2011 0.02 % 2012 to 2015	0	0	0	30	30	30	30	40	40	40	40	**280**
Terra Tax (imposed on a trade volume of US$ 8.5 trillion billion): 0.35 % 2008 to 2011 0.50 % 2012 to 2015	0	0	0	29.7	29.7	29.7	29.7	42.4	42.4	42.4	42.4	**288**
Total		68	68	158	158	158	158	190	190	190	190	**1,528**
Additionally raised funds until 2015 (billion US $)												**978**

Concluding Remarks

The schedule for a **Global Marshall Plan / Planetary Contract is ambitious**. However, the worldwide problems do indeed require such an ambitious step. The point of departure is favorable, as many of the respective global measures, agreements and forms of action can almost readily be joined together like the pieces of a **jigsaw puzzle** as soon as theblockades of game theoretical nature are overcome, negotiated applying an eco-social approach.

The latter provides a **novel design** for a future **global governance system**, with further **market openings** by the rich countries, and **co-financing** in return for the willingness to accept standards at its core. While the present individual regimes like the ILO had to be elaborated and many difficult detail provisions made over many years of development, the integration of different regimes to be accomplished now is much easier in terms of design and the **amount of documentation required**. Provided that there is a willingness to make a "deal", this task can be specified and implemented within a short timeframe.

The Global Marshall Plan / Planetary Contract Initiative pursues this goal forcefully. The broad approval from prominent personages from politics, private enterprise, and science, but also from groups from all parts of society, was a great encouragement for all of the involved (for details refer to addendum 2). This approval must be seized and the endeavors must not ease up. A great deal is at stake - the beneficial future of the globe [91].

Acknowledgements / To this text

If it had not been for the close cooperation and intensive interaction with many partners sustaining the Global Marshall Plan Initiative, the text at hand would not exist in this form. This includes in particular many of the young generation who attend to questions regarding the future within the respective foundations and NGOs.

The support from members of the following organizations was of particular importance (in alphabetical order): AIESEC, Attac, Breuninger Foundation, Club of Budapest, Club of Rome, Committee for a democratic UN, Eco-social Forum Europe, Federal Association for Business Promotion and Foreign Trade, Foundation Apfelbaum, Foundation Kathy Beys, German Association of the Junior Chamber International, German Branch of Friends of the Earth (BUND), German Environmental Management Association (B.A.U.M), Global Contract Foundation, Global Marshall Plan Foundation, Global Society Dialogue of the former EU Information Society Forum, Protestant Academy Tutzing, Institute for Environmental Management Berlin, Rotarian Initiative for Population & Development (RIFPD), Terra One World Network, University.Club Klagenfurt, University of Stuttgart, World Future Council (under construction), the EU project TERRA 2000 on globalization and sustainable development, Youth for Intergenerational Justice and Sustainability (YOIS), and all colleagues involved at the FAW in Ulm.

Further mention should be made of all individuals and organizations who participated in the meetings of the Initiative for World Peace, Sustainability and Equity on May 16, 2003 in Frankfurt, on November 14/15, 2003 in Haus Rissen/Hamburg, on January 29/30, 2004, and May 04/05, 2004 in Brussels. Special thanks to Frithjof Finkbeiner, an untiring and effective fighter and organizer for the Initiative, and the professional and dedicated team of the Initiative's office in Haus Rissen, Hamburg, for its indispensable support; named in representation: Helge Bork and Maike Sippel.

To be explicitly mentioned, in alphabetical order:
Franz Alt (Journalist), Elnara Babayeva (Global Contract Foundation), Josip Baotic (Eco-social Forum Croatia), Joachim Berger (TGM), Maritta von Bieberstein Koch-Weser (GEXSI), HRH Prinz El Hassan bin Talal (Club of Rome), Carl Eduard von Bismarck (BWA), Susanne Boehncke (Boehncke PR), Klaus Boldt (Journalist), Andrew Bollinger (EPEA), Leo Borchardt (Club Ad Fundum), Arnaud Bordet (Global Contract Foundation), Helge Bork (Global Contract Foundation), Fritz Brickwedde (Deutsche Bundesstiftung Umwelt), Andreas Bummel (Committee for a Democratic U.N.), Ulrich Dettweiler (Protestant Academy Tutzing), Guido Eberhard (Attac), Peter Eigen (Transparency International), Udo Eitzenberger (Eitzenberger, Media Print Logistics), Adolfo Perez Esquivel (Nobel Prize of Peace), Edwin Ferger (E. Ferger publishing house), Peter Fernau (Club of Budapest), Frithjof Finkbeiner (Global Contract Foundation), Karolin Finkbeiner (Global Marshall Plan Foundation), Birgit Franzen (Coralis Software), Klaudius Gansczyk (Society for Intercultural Cooperation), Maximilian Gege (B.A.U.M. e. V.), Jens Geiger (Global Contract Foundation), Hans-Dietrich Genscher (Former Foreign Minister), Susan George (Transnational Institute), Bridget Gillaspy (Global Contract Foundation), Friedemann Greiner (Protestantic Academy Tutzing), Nicole Gronewald (Global Contract Foundation), Horst Gross (University.Club Klagenfurt), Thomas Häringer (State Parliament Baden-Württemberg at the EU), Dieter Härthe (Federal Association for Economic Advancement and Foreign Trade (BWA), Katie Halcrow (Global Contract Foundation), Karl Peter Hasenkamp (Theodor Heuss Academy Gummersbach), W. Heidrich (Research Center Jülich), Andreas Henschel (Federal Association for Business Promotion and Foreign Trade), Klaus Herbert (TGM), Peter Hesse (Peter-Hesse-Foundation), Manfred Höhl (Fraunhofer Services, Berlin), Hans-Herbert Holzamer (Süddeutsche

Zeitung), Wolfram Huncke (BWI, München), Michael Ihden (Coralis Software), Peter Johnston (EU Commission), Thomas Kämpke (FAW Ulm), Reinhard Kappe (Brot für die Welt, Stuttgart), Alexander Karim (Coralis Software), Stephen Karnik (Bahá'í International Community), Prof. Milan Konecny (World Cartographic Society, Brno), Melissa Kostelecky (Global Contract Foundation), Andrea von Lehmden (Global Contract Foundation), Ervin Laszlo (Club of Budapest), Sabine Leidig (attac), Claire Louiset (Global Contract Foundation), Andreas May (Global Contract Foundation), Eike Messow (Breuniger Foundation), Uwe Möller (Club of Rome), Markus Neuhoff (Global Contract Foundation), Hartmut Nowotny (Terra One World Net), Christian Osterhaus (Welthungerhilfe), Jörn Paessler (Paessler Publishing), Katharina Peisker (YOIS), Katja Pfeiffer (YOIS), Nicanor Perlas (alternative Nobel Prize), Gerd Pfitzenmaier (Ausdruck publishing house), Maartje van Putten (Inspection Panel World Bank), Monika Rahm (Global Contract Foundation), Josef Riegler (Eco-social Forum Europe), Wolfgang Riehn (Yehudi Menuin Foundation), Alain Rivière (EPEA), Jörn Rosebrock (Global Contract Foundation), Michael Rügge (Global Contract Foundation), Ilja Sallacz (Agentur Liquid), Thomas Schauer (European Support Centre of the Club of Rome, Vienna), Ernst Scheiber (Eco-social Forum Austria), Helge and Hans Martin Scheuch (Rotarian Fellowship on Population and Development), Josef Schmaus (Outline - Online Medien GmbH), Annemarie and Peter Schrott, Luísa Schmidt (Expresso), Jakob Schoof (YOIS), Dietmar Schwarzenbacher (Uniquare, Krumpendorf), Irmgard Schwaetzer (Friedrich Naumann Foundation), Maike Sippel (Global Contract Foundation), Surjo R. Soekadar (project leader for the Initiative on behalf of the Global Contract Foundation), Dirk Sonnenschein (Coralis Software), Peter Spiegel (Club of Budapest), R. K. Stappen (Franz von Assisi Academy for the protection of the Earth e. V.), Markus Stark (FAW Ulm), Sabine Stoeck (Global Contract Foundation), Sumiko Tanaka (Global Contract Foundation), Mark Tercha (Global Contract Foundation), Oliver Tschirdewahn (activemeta), Jakob von Uexküll (World Future Council), Christopher Wagner

(FH Stralsund), Ernst Ulrich von Weizsäcker (Club of Rome), Raoul Weiler (Club of Rome), Lutz Wicke (Institute for Environmental Management Berlin), Anders Wijkman (Club of Rome), George Winter (INEM), Angelika Zahrnt (BUND), Horst W. Zillmer (Foundation Children in Africa) and Robert Zinser (Rotarian Fellowship on Population and Development).

From the scientific side, I thank my colleagues Wolfgang Eichhorn (TU Karlsruhe) and Joachim Voeller (Universität Ulm) for their help on detail questions, Rolf H. Möhring (TU Berlin) for a continuous exchange on the topic, and eminently Paul Stähly (University St. Gallen), who for years and especially in the last months has lent his very intensive support to the work on these reflections.

I wish to thank the Eco-Social Forum Europe and its president, former vice-chancellor Dr. Josef Riegler and the Secretary General, Prof. Ernst Scheiber, for again mustering the vision, motivation and organizational strength to publish this report and support its translation and publication in other languages.

Thanks to my secretary Sabine Grau and co-workers, particularly Regina Simon, for their patience and unrelenting dedication and professionalism in supporting the difficult creation process of this text.

Thanks to Bettina Hofstaetter for the English Translation and to Gudrun Gusel for the professional lectorship.

For a very professional work carried out under considerable time pressure a special thanks to the coordination office Global Marshall Plan, Hamburg, Germany.

Finally, I am indebted to my colleague and comrade-in-arms Robert Pestel (EU-Commission, † 18 April 2003), who has left us much too early, and without whom, these reflections would not exist in the form they have today.

List of Abbreviations

ADB	Asian Development Bank
CDM	Clean Development Mechanism
DAC	Development Assistant Committee
EBRD	European Bank for Reconstruction and Development
FAO	Food and Agriculture Organization of the United Nations
GDP	Gross Domestic Product
GEA	Global Environmental Agency
IDB	Inter-American Development Bank
IFC	International Finance Corporation
IFCCC	International Framework Convention on Climate Change
ILO	International Labour Organization
IPWSKM	International compact on the economic, social and cultural human rights
IMF	International Monetary Fund
OESO-DAC Norms	Statistics from OESO and DAC
OPEC	Organization of the Petroleum Exporting Countries
PRSP	Poverty Reduction Strategy Paper
UN	United Nations
UNDP	United Nations Development Program
UNEP	United Nations Environmental Program
UNESCO	United Nations Education, Scientific and Cultural Organization
UNFCCC	UN Convention on Climate Change
UNFPA	United Nations Population Fund
UNICEF	United Nations Children Fund
WB	World Bank
WSIS	World Summit on the Information Society
WSSD	World Summit on Sustainable Development
WTO	World Trade Organization

Bibliography

1. Affemann, N., B.F. Pelz and F.J. Radermacher:
Globale Herausforderungen und Bevölkerungsentwicklung: Die Menschheit ist bedroht.
Beitrag für den Beirat der Deutschen Stiftung Weltbevölkerung e. V.. Landesstelle Baden-Württemberg, 1997

2. Alt, F. et al.:
Aktion "Globale Umweltpartnerschaft" - Aufruf zu einem "Ökologischen Marshallplan". Berlin, 1997

3. Annan, K. (ed.):
Brücken in die Zukunft - Ein Manifest für den Dialog der Kulturen. S. Fischer, Frankfurt am Main, 2001
[Annan, K. (ed.): Dialogue among civilizations: The Round Table on the Eve of the United Nations Millennium Summit. Paris, 2001]

4. Annan, K.:
Der UNvollendete Weg - Die Vereinten Nationen im 21.Jahrhundert. Hamburg, 2003
[Annan, K.: We the Peoples: The Role of the United Nations in the 21st Century. New York, 2000]

5. Annan, K.:
UN Secretary General's Message for New Year, 2004, www.un.org/News/Press/docs/2003/sgsm9095.doc.htm

6. Andersen, N. S.:
Bericht der ILO-Weltkommission zur sozialen Dimension der Globalisierung. Newsletter of Global Contract Foundation, 1/2004

7. Bartosch, U. and J. Wagner (eds.):
Weltinnenpolitik. Zur Theorie des Friedens von Carl Friedrich von Weizsäcker. LIT Verlag, Münster, 1998

8. Baus, R. T. and U. von Wilamowitz-Moellendorff:
Globalisierungsdebatte III: ATTAC - Die neue außerparlamentarische Opposition? Arbeitspapiere der Konrad Adenauer Stiftung e.V.. Nr. 124, 2004

9. Behrendt, S. and U. Gartzke:
Auf der Suche nach einer neuen globalen Ordnung. Davos 2004, Internationale Politik, 2/2004

10. Braungart, M. and McDonough, W.:
Einfach intelligent produzieren. BvT Berliner Taschenbuch Verlags GmbH, Berlin, 2003

11. Braungart, M., R. Ketelhut and A. Rivière.:
Eco-effective design of products and production systems - Eight theses on methodological and institutional prerequisites.

12. Brown, G.: Tackling Poverty:
A Global New Deal. A Modern Marshall Plan for The Developing World, Pamphlet based on the speeches to the New York Federal Reserve, 16 November 2001, and the Press Club, Washington D.C.. 17 December 2001. HM Treasury, February 2002

13. Brown, G.:
Speech by the Chancellor of the Exchequer Gordon Brown at the conference on "Making Globalisation Work For All - The Challenge Of Delivering The Monterrey Consensus, London, 16 February 2004, The full text of the speech can be found at:
http://www.hm-treasury.gov.uk/Newsroom_and_Speeches/Press/2004/press_12_04.cfm

14. Brunnhuber, S. and H. Klimenta:
Wie wir wirtschaften werden. Szenarien und Gestaltungsmöglichkeiten für zukunftsfähige Finanzmärkte. Redline Wirtschaft bei ueberreuter, Frankfurt/Wien, 2003

15. Bundesministerium für wirtschaftliche Zusammenarbeit und Entwicklung (ed.):
BMZ Spezial: Sexuelle und reproduktive Gesundheit (SRG). Positionspapier des BMZ, 2003

16. Camerer, C. and R. Thaler:
Ultimatums, dictators, and manners. J. of Economic Perspectives 9, 209-219, 1995

17. de Soto, H.:
The Mystery of Capital: Why Capitalism Triumphs in the West and Fails Everywhere Else. Basic Books, New York, 2000

18. Deutsche Stiftung Weltbevölkerung,
diverse material on world population growth, www.dsw-online.de

19. Deutsche Stiftung Weltbevölkerung:
DSW newsletter 6/2003, www.dsw-online.de

20. Devarajan, S. (HDNVP), M. J. Miller (HDNVP and SRM) and E. V. Swanson (DECDG):
Goals for Development: History, Prospects and Costs, April 2002 (Study of the Worldbank)

21. Dürr, H.-P.:
Für eine zivile Gesellschaft. Beiträge zu unserer Zukunftsfähigkeit. dtv Taschenbuch, München, 2002

22. Eberhard, G.:
Thoughts on a new Consensus. Personal communication, 2004

23. El Hassan bin Talal:
Third Environmental Forum, Global Foresight Lecture. DaimlerChrysler Environmental Symposium, Magdeburg, 17 November 2003

24. epd (Evangelischer Pressedienst):
Phoenix aus der Asche: Die Tobin-Steuer wird den Weltsozialgipfel beschäftigen. Entwicklungspolitik 9/10/2000, www.epd.de

25. FAO (ed.):
The State of Food Insecurity of the World 2003, www.fao.org/DOCREP/006/J0083E/J0083E00.HTM

26. Fay, M. and T. Yepes:
Investing in Infrastructure. What is Needed from 2000 to 2010?. The World Bank Policy Research Working Paper 3102, July 2003

27. Forum Informationsgesellschaft (ed.):
Informationsgesellschaft, Globalisierung und nachhaltige Entwicklung - Perspektiven für einen europäisch-inspirierten Weg. Bielefeld, 2000

28. Gansczyk, K.:
Zukunftsfähige Visionen in der Bildungspraxis. In: Hintersteiner, N., N.Nakamura and H.J. Scheidgen (Ed.), Philosophie, Gesellschaft und Bildung in Zeiten der Globalisierung Amsterdam, Rodopi, 2003

29. Gege, M.:
"Die Zukunftsanleihe" - Ein Modell für Deutschlands Weg aus der Krise. München, Ökom, 2004

30. Geiss, J., D. Wortmann and Zuber, F. (eds.):
Nachhaltige Entwicklung - Strategie für das 21. Jahrhundert?. Leske + Budrich, Opladen, 2003

31. George, S.:
Clusters of Crisis and a Planetary Contract. Budapest, 18 October 2001, www.tni.org/archives/george/clusters.htm

32. George, S.:
Attac Frankreich diskutiert den Globalen Marshall Plan, www.attac.org, www.tni.org/george

33. Global Society Dialogue, www.global-society-dialogue.org

34. Gorbachev, M. / Gorbatschow, M.:
Mein Manifest für die Erde - Jetzt handeln für Frieden, globale Gerechtigkeit und eine ökologische Zukunft. Campus, Frankfurt/New York, 2003
[Gorbachev, M.: Mandate for Peace, PaperJacks, 1997]

35. Gore, A.: Wege zum Gleichgewicht - Ein Marshallplan für die Erde. S. Fischer Verlag GmbH, Frankfurt, 1992
[Gore, A.: Earth in the Balance: Ecology and the Human Spirit. Boston, 2000]

36. Gore, A.: The Digital Earth:
Understanding our planet in the 21st Century, speach delivered at the California Science Center, Los Angeles, California, on January 31, 1998, www.digitalearth.gov/VP19980131.html

37. Gorz, A.: Misère du présent - richesse du possible.
Galilée, Paris, 1997

38. Grefe, Ch., M. Greffrath, and H. Schumann: Attac
- Was wollen die Globalisierungskritiker?, Rowohlt-Berlin Verlag GmbH, Berlin, 2002

39. Hamburgisches Welt-Wirtschafts-Archiv (ed.):
Jahresbericht 2002. Hamburg, 2002

40. Hasenkamp, K. P.:
Sanierung des Globus, Theodor-Heuss-Akademie, Gummersbach, Seminar Erdpolitik, Februar 1992, Programm-Vorschlag zur Sanierung des Globus. Vortrag 12.02.1992

41. Hawrylyshyn, B.:
Road Maps to the Future, Towards more effective societies, A Report to the Club of Rome. Pergamon Press, Oxford, 1980

42. Hefeker, C.:
Handels- und Finanzarchitektur im Umbruch: Globale Integration und die institutionelle Arbeitsteilung von IWF, Weltbank und WTO. HWWA Discussion Paper 225, Hamburg Institute of International Economics, 2003

43. Heidrich, W.: Personal communication, 2004

44. Hengsbach, F.:
Gegen Unmenschlichkeit in der Wirtschaft - Der Hirtenbrief der Katholischen Bischöfe der USA "Wirtschaftliche Gerechtigkeit für alle". Herder, Freiburg, Basel, Wien, 1987

45. Hesse, P.:
Wirksamer Mitteleinsatz zur nachhaltigen Heilung globaler Missstände und Ungerechtigkeiten, insbesondere im Rahmen des Konzeptes eines globalen Marshallplans,
Konzeptionelle Anregungen aus der Praxis.
Peter-Hesse-Stiftung, Kaarst-Büttgen, Germany, 2004, www.solidarity.org

46. Hettlage, R.:
Die anthropologische Konzeption des Genossenschaftswesens, Theorie und Praxis - Welche Chance hat der "homo cooperativus"?
In: Laurinkari (ed.) Genossenshaftswesen.
Oldenbourg Verlag, München/Wien, S. 40, 1990

47. ILO-Report: www.ilo.org/wcsdg

48. Information Society Forum (ed.):
The European Way for the Information Society.
European Commission, Brussels, 2000

49. International Labour Organization (ILO) (ed.):
Report of the Director-General: Appendix, Report on the situation of worker of the occupied Arab territories. International Labour Conference, 90th Session, 6/2002, International Labour Office, Geneva, ISBN 92-2-112426-6

50. International Monetary Fund:
Financing the Fund´s Operations - Review of Issues.
April 2001; www.imf.org

51. International Planned Parenthood Federation:
http:\\www.ippf.org

52. International Programme on the Elimination of Child Labour (IPEC):
Investing In Every Child - An Economic Study of the Costs and Benefits of Elimintating Child Labour. International Labour Office, Geneva, December 2003

53. Johnston, P.:
Comments on the proposed Global Marshall Plan,
05-02-04, personal communication

54. Kapitza, S. P.:
Global Population Blow-Up and After.
Information Society and the Demographic Revolution. 2003.
Available at sergey@kapitza.ras.ru

55. Kaul, I., P. Conceição, K. Le Goulven and R. U. Mendoza (eds.): Bereitstellung globaler öffentlicher Güter. Globalisierung gestalten. UNDP Entwicklungsprogramm der Vereinten Nationen. New York, Oxford, Oxford University Press, 2003
[Kaul, I., P. Conceição, K. Le Goulven and R. U. Mendoza (eds.): Providing Global Public Goods: Managing Globalization, New York: New York: Oxford University Press, 2002]

56. Khor, M.:
Globalisierung gerechter gestalten. NWWP-Verlag, Stuttgart, 2002
[Khor, M.: Rethinking Globalization: Critical Issues and Policy Choices. London, Zed Books, 2001]

57. Kleinwächter, W.:
Auf dem Weg zum UN Weltgipfel der Informationsgesellschaft (WSIS): Ein Tagebuch. Published in: Global Contract Watch. 2003, www.weltvertrag.org

58. Koch, J.:
Megaphilosophie. Das Freiheitsversprechen der Ökonomie. Steidl Taschenbuch 182, Göttingen, 2003

59. Köhler, H.:
Orientierung für eine bessere Globalisierung, Öffentliche Antrittsvorlesung anlässlich der Verleihung der Honorarprofessur an der Eberhard Karls Universität zu Tübingen, 16.10.2003

60. Konecny, M.:
The Digital Earth: Spatial Data Infrastructures from Local to Global Concept. In Proceedings on the Int. Symposium on Digital Earth, "Towards the Digital Earth", Beijing, 1999

61. Konecny, M. (ed.):
Proceedings "Digital Earth - Information Resources for Global Sustainability" conference, 21.-25.09.2003, Brno, Czech Republic. Introduction, Masavyk University Brno, 2003

62. Küng, H.:
Projekt Weltethos. 2. Aufl., Piper Verlag, München, 1993

63. Küng, H.:
Weltethos für Weltpolitik und Weltwirtschaft. Piper Verlag, München, 1997

64. Küng, H. (ed.):
Globale Unternehmen - globales Ethos. Frankfurter Allgemeine Buch, Frankfurt, 2001

65. Küng, H. and D. Senghaas (ed.):
Friedenspolitik: Ethische Grundlagen internationaler Beziehungen. Piper, München, 2003

66. Lebensministerium.at (ed.):
Ways towards Sustainability in the European Union - beyond the European Spring, Summit 2003, Schriftenreihe des BMLFUW, Band 9/2003, Republik Österreich, Bundesministerium für Land- und Forstwirtschaft, Umwelt und Wasserwirtschaft, November 2003

67. Maier-Rigaud, F. P. and G. Maier-Rigaud:
Das neoliberale Projekt. Metropolis-Verlag Marburg, 2001, S. 201-306

68. Merry, P.:
Strategies for Bridging Global Gaps. A Report from the Forum 2000 Conference 2003. www.naturaldesign.nl/articles.html

69. Mesarovic, M. D., R. Pestel and F. J. Radermacher:
Which Future? Manuscript to the EU Project TERRA 2000. FAW, Ulm, 2003

70. Möller, U., F. J. Radermacher, J. Riegler, S. R. Soekadar and P. Spiegel:
Global Marshall Plan: Das Ende von Armut und Umweltzerstörung durch eine globale öko-soziale Marktwirtschaft. More Information at www.globalmarshallplan.org. Horizonte Verlag, July 2004

71. Moser, A. and J. Riegler:
Konfrontation oder Versöhnung? Ökosoziale Politik mit der Weisheit der Natur! Leopold Stocker Verlag, Graz, Stuttgart, 2001

72. Nachhaltigkeitsbeirat Baden-Württemberg (NBBW):
Nachhaltiger Klimaschutz durch Initiativen und Innovationen aus Baden-Württemberg. Sondergutachten, Stuttgart, 2003

73. Neirynck, J.:
Der göttliche Ingenieur. expert-Verlag, Renningen, 1994

74. Odysseum Köln (ed.):
Odysseum Köln - Leben. Wissen. Zukunft. Publikumsbroschüre, 2004

75. Odysseum Köln (ed.):
Odysseum Köln - Leben. Wissen. Zukunft. Partnerinformation, 2004

76. Österreichische Industriellen Vereinigung:
Österreich.Nachhaltig.Gestalten - Die IV-Zukunftsstrategie für Wirtschaft, Politik und Gesellschaft.Industriellenvereinigung, Schwarzenbergplatz 4, 1031 Wien, Juni 2003

77. Ott, E., T. Santarius and A. Heym:
Sustainable Governance, Globale Umwelt- und Nachhaltigkeitspolitik am Beginn des 21. Jahrhunderts. Wuppertal Institut, 2003

78. Pestel, R. and F. J. Radermacher:
Equity, Wealth and Growth: Why Market Fundmentalism Makes Countries Poor. Manuscript to the EU Project TERRA 2000, FAW, Ulm, 2003

79. Pestel, R. and F. J. Radermacher:
ICT and Sustainability: Is there a Chance? Manuscript to the EU Project TERRA 2000. FAW, Ulm, 2003

80. van Putten, M.:
Personal Communication, 2004

81. Radermacher, F. J.:
Globalisierung und Informationstechnologie. In: Weltinnenpolitik, Intern. Tagung anlässlich des 85. Geburtstages von Carl-Friedrich von Weizsäcker, Evangelische Akademie Tutzing, 1997. U. Bartosch and J. Wagner (eds.). LIT Verlag, Münster, 1998, S. 105-117

82. Radermacher, F. J.:
Hoffnungen: Zukunftsfragen der Menschheit - Problembereiche, Lösungsansätze und Hinweise zu 20 Hoffnung-machenden Initiativen. Manuskript, Ulm, 1999

83. Radermacher, F. J.:
Globalisierung, Bevölkerungsentwicklung und Nachhaltigkeit: Herausforderungen für die Gesellschaft und die Rolle von ROTARY. Sonderdruck Interdistriktskonferenz 2000 (Distrikt 1980 und 2000), Luzern/Schweiz, 2000

84. Radermacher, F. J. (ed.):
Informationsgesellschaft und nachhaltige Entwicklung. Wissensverarbeitung und Gesellschaft. Universitäts-Verlag, Ulm GmbH, 2000

85. Radermacher, F. J.:
New Economy. Börsenrausch und Greencard: Spielt die Welt verrückt oder hat alles seine Logik? in: Wohin geht die Wissensgesellschaft?, R. Rüdel and C. Stadelhofer (eds.). Kleine Verlag, Bielefeld, 2002, Band 9, S. 80-128

86. Radermacher, F. J.:
Die neue Zukunftsformel. Bild der Wissenschaft, Heft 4/2002, S. 78-86, April 2002

87. Radermacher, F. J.:
Balance oder Zerstörung: Ökosoziale Marktwirtschaft als Schlüssel zu einer weltweiten nachhaltigen Entwicklung. Ecosocial Forum Europe (ed.), Franz Josefs-Kai 13, A-1010 Wien, August 2002
[Radermacher, F.J.: Balance or Destruction: Ecosocial Market Economy as the Key to Global Sustainabel Development. Ecosocial Forum Europe (ed.), Vienna, 2004
both versions available, via fax +49(0)4082090421 or at: www.globalmarshallplan.org

88. Radermacher, F. J.:
Herausforderungen an den Standort Deutschland (2003): Keine einfachen Zeiten. Textmanuskript, FAW, Ulm, 2003

89. Radermacher, F. J.:
Die Zukunft der Wirtschaft: Nachhaltigkeitskonformes Wachstum, sozialer Ausgleich, kulturelle Balance und Ökologie. Tagung des Universitäts.Clubs Klagenfurt, Abbazia di Rosazzo, Friul/Italy, 2003

90. Radermacher, F. J.:
Application of the Terra 2000 results: towards the Global Marshall Plan. Manuscript to the EU Project TERRA 2000, FAW, Ulm, 2003

91. Radermacher, F. J. and S. Wehsener:
The Globalization Saga. Balance or Destruction - Balance oder Zerstörung. Storybook (ISBN 3-89559-260-9), Video und CD zum Musical. FAW, Ulm, 2003. available via facsimile to 0731 501-111 or at radermacher@faw.uni-ulm.de

92. Report of the National Energy Policy Development Group: Reliable, Affordable, and Environmentally Sound - Energy for America's Future. Washington, May 16th, 2001, U.S Government Printing Office, http://bookstore.gpo.gov/, ISBN 0-16-050814-2

93. Riegler, J.: Anworten auf die Zukunft, Ökosoziale Marktwirtschaft 1990. Adolf Holzhausens Nfg., Vienna, ISBN 3-900-518-05-X

94. Rotarian Fellowship Population and Development. See www.rfpd.de; for more information, please contact Past-Gov. Robert Zinser (robert.zinser@t-online.de)

95. Rüstow, A. Das Versagen des Wirtschaftsliberalismus. Metropolis-Verlag Marburg, 2001, S. 19-200

96. Sabet, H.: Die "Terra-Tax" oder: Wie kann man einen weltweiten sozialen Marshallplan fast zum Nulltarif finanzieren? www.terra-network.de/change-tax-sabet.htm

97. Sachs, W.: Ökologie und Menschenrechte. Wuppertal Paper Nr. 131, Wuppertal Institute for Climate, Environment, Energy, 2003

98. Santarius, T., H. Dalkmann, M. Steigenberger and K. Vogelpohl: Grüne Grenzen für den Welthandel. Wuppertal Paper Nr. 133, Wuppertal Institute for Climate, Environment, Energy, 2003

99. Schauer, T. and F. J. Radermacher (eds.): The Challenge of the Digital Divide. 2001. ISBN 3-89559-236-6. For more information, see www.global-society-dialogue.org

100. Schmidt, H. (ed.): Allgemeine Erklärung der Menschenpflichten - Ein Vorschlag. Piper Verlag GmbH, München, 1997

101. Schmidt, H.: Globalisierung. Deutsche Verlags-Anstalt Stuttgart, 1998

102. Schmidt-Bleek, F.: Wieviel Umwelt braucht der Mensch? MIPS - Das Maß für ökologisches Wirtschaften. Birkhäuser Verlag, 1993

103. Schwarz, P. and D. Randall: An Abrupt Climate Change Scenario and its Implications for United States National Security. October 2003, www.ems.org/climate/pentagon_climate_change.html and www.stopesso.com/campaign/00000143.php

104. Sen, A.: Ökonomie für den Menschen. Wege zur Gerechtigkeit und Solidarität in der Marktwirtschaft. Carl Hanser Verlag, 2000

105. S. Dejaveran, HDNVP, M. J. Miller, HDNVP and SRM, E. V. Swanson, DECDG: Goals for Development: History, Prospects and Costs. April 2002

106. Social Watch Deutschland (ed.): Die Armen und der Markt. Report 2003, info@eed.de

107. Sontag, S.:
Regarding the Pain of Others. Farrar, Straus & Giroux, New York, 2003

108. Soros, G.:
Die Krise des globalen Kapitalismus. Offene Gesellschaft in Gefahr. Alexander Fest Verlag, Berlin, 1998

109. Soros, G.:
Der Globalisierungs-Report. Weltwirtschaft auf dem Prüfstand. Alexander Fest Verlag, Berlin, 2001
[Soros, G.: George Soros on Globalization. New York, 2002]

110. Späth, L.:
Die Change-the-World-Tax. Wegweiser zu einer weltweit sozialen Marktwirtschaft. Laudation auf Muhammad Yunus anlässlich der Verleihung des "Planetary Consciousness Award" des Club of Budapest am 25. Juni 1997 in der Frankfurter Paulskirche

111. Spiegel, P.:
TERRA TAX: Die neue Finanzierungsquelle. www.club-of-budapest.com/cob_d/Publikationen/ pub-terra-tax-d.pdf

112. Stappen, R. K.:
Die Global Marshall Plan Initiative und der Rio-Johannesburg Prozess, Strategische Optionen für die Umsetzung. Franz von Assisi Akademie zum Schutz der Erde e. V., Eichstätt, 2004

113. Stiftung für die Rechte zukünftiger Generationen / Foundation for the Rights of Future Generations (ed.):
"Ihr habt dieses Land nur von uns geborgt...". Rasch u. Röhring Verlag, Hamburg, 1997

114. Stiftung für die Rechte zukünftiger Generationen / Foundation for the Rights of Future Generations (ed.):
Handbuch Generationengerechtigkeit. ökom Verlag, 2003

115. Stiglitz, J.E.:
Die Schatten der Globalisierung. Siedler, Berlin, 2002

116. Streminger, G.:
Markt, Motive, Moralische Institutionen - Zur Philosophie Adam Smiths. revised edition March 2004, first published in "Archiv für Geschichte der Philosophie", 74. Band 1992 Heft 3, hg. v. Rainer Specht, Verlag Walter De Gruyter, Berlin - New York, S. 272-302

117. The Earth Charter Initiative (ed.):
The Earth Charter. Costa Rica, 2000; www.earthcharter.org

118. The World Bank (ed.):
Millennium Development Goals. Report No. 24613, 2002

119. The World Bank:
The World Bank and Civil Society Organizations:
Issues and Options for Improving Institutional Engagement: A Discussion Paper. Civil Society Team, External Affairs Department and Social Development Department, The World Bank, Oct. 2002

120. Tobin Tax Initiative
For more information, please see www.ceedweb.org/iirp/121

Trans-Mediterranean Renewable Energy Cooperation "TREC":
A Powerful Partnership for Development, Climate Stabilisation and Good Neighbourhood. Arab Thought Forum, Amman, 2003.
For more information, please see
http://saharawind.com/documents/trec.paper.pdf

122. Transparency International:
For more information, see www.transparency.org/

123. UNFPA (ed.):
Reproductive Health, Family Planning and Population Promote Millennium Development Goals. In: State of the World. Population 2002 - People, Poverty and Possibilities, 2002

124. United Nations Department of Public Information:
Implementing the Millennium Declaration. Goal 8: Development of global partnership for development, October 2002. www.unmillennium-project.org

125. United Nations Department of Public Information:
Implementing the Millennium Declaration. Regional Charts, October 2002. www.unmillenniumproject.org

126. United Nations Development Program:
The Millennium Development Compact. www.undp.org/hdr2003/pdf/hdr03_MDC.pdf

127. United Nations Division for Sustainable Development (ed.):
Indicators of Sustainable Development: Guidelines and Methodologies www.un.org/esa/sustdev/natlinfo/indicators/indisd/indisd-mg2001.pdf

128. United Nations General Assembly:
Implementation of the United Nations Millennium Declaration. Report of the Secretary-General, A/58/323, 2 September 2003

129. United Nations Non-Governmental Liaison Service (NGLS):
Go between, No. 101, December-January 2004

130. Universitäts.Club Klagenfurt (ed.):
Friulanisches Manifest. [Friuli Manifesto]. Friul/Klagenfurt, 2003

131. Vehmas, J., P. Malaska, J. Luukkanen, J. Kaivo-oja, O. Hietanen, M. Vinnari and J. Ilvonen:
Europe in Global Battle of Sustainability: Rebound Strikes Back? Advanced Sustainability Analysis. Series Discussion and Working Papers 7, Turku School of Economics and Business Administration, 2003

132. von Uexkuell, J.:
for a World Future Council. http:\\www.worldfuturecouncil.org or www.weltzukunftsrat.de

133. von Weizsäcker, C. F.:
Bedingungen des Friedens. Vandenhoeck und Ruprecht, Göttingen, 1964

134. von Weizsäcker, E. U., A. B. Lovins and L. H. Lovins:
Faktor Vier: doppelter Wohlstand, halbierter Naturverbrauch. Droemer-Knaur, 1995

[von Weizsäcker, E. U., A. B. Lovins and L. H. Lovins: Factor Four: Doubling Wealth - Halving Resource Use: The New Report to the Club of Rome. Earthscan. London, 1996]

135. von Weizsäcker, E. U., O. Young and M. Finger:
Limits to Privatisation - How to Avoid Too Much of a Good Thing, to be published 2004

136. Wicke, L. and J. Knebel:
Nachhaltige Klimaschutzpolitik durch weltweite ökonomische Anreize zum Klimaschutz. Studie im Auftrag des Ministeriums für Umwelt und Verkehr des Landes Baden-Württemberg, Berlin/Stuttgart, September 2003

137. Wicke, L. and J. Knebel: GCCS:
Nachhaltige Klimaschutzpolitik durch ein markt- und anreizorientiertes Globales Klima-Zertifikats-System. Studie im Auftrag des Ministeriums für Umwelt und Verkehr des Landes Baden-Württemberg, Berlin/Stuttgart, Dezember 2003

138. von Wilamowitz-Moellendorff, U. (ed.):
Globalisierungsdebatte II: Positionen und Gegenpositionen. Zukunftsforum Politik der Konrad Adenauer Stiftung e. V., Nr. 54, 2003

139. Windfuhr, M.:
Parallelbericht Menschenrechte. Deutschlands Erfüllung seiner internationalen Verpflichtungen gemäß dem Internationalen Pakt über wirtschaftliche, soziale und kulturelle Menschenrechte (IPWSKM).
Im Auftrag von Brot für die Welt und Evangelischer Entwicklungsdienst e.V. (EED), Bonn, Stuttgart, Heidelberg, 2001

140. Winpenny, J.:
Financing water for all. Third World Water Forum, March 2003, ISBN 92-95017-01-3

141. Witzsch, G.:
Von Rio nach Kyoto. Die großen Umweltkonferenzen der Vereinten Nationen in den 90er Jahren. Waxmann Verlag GmbH, Münster, 1999

142. Wohlmeyer, H. (ed.):
The WTO, Agriculture and Sustainable Development.
Österreichische Vereinigung für Agrarwissenschaftliche Forschung, Wien, 2002

143. World Health Organisation (ed.):
A Research Policy Agenda for Science and Technology to support Global Health Development. WHO Collaborating Center for Global Modelling of Health Perspectives, Günzburg, Germany, 1998, ISBN 3-00-003371-8

144. YOIS (ed.):
What's next? The Future of the Information Society - a Youth Perspective. Stuttgart, 2003

145. Yunus, M.:
Grameen - Eine Bank für die Armen der Welt,
Lübbe, 1999
[Yunus, M.: Grameen - a bank for the poor. Grameen Bank. Dhaka, 1986]

146. Ziegler, J.:
Die neuen Herrscher der Welt und ihre globalen Widersacher.
C. Bertelsmann Verlag, 2003

147. Zillmer, H. W.:
Die Zukunft beginnt heute... und wohin gehst Du, Homo sapiens?
Wege zu einer nachhaltig tragfähigen globalen Entwicklung.
Verlag Dr. Hans-Dieter Höhnk, Reinbek, 1999

148. Zittel, W. and M. Treber:
Analysis of BP Statistical Review of World Energy with Respect to CO_2 Emissions. Joint Working Paper,
Ludwig-Bölkow-Systemtechnik GmbH, Ottobrunn (www.lbst.de) und Germanwatch, Bonn (www.germanwatch.org), July 2003

Addendum 1

Executive Summary: Considerations on a Global Marshall Plan

As a consequence of rapid globalization, the world is in a difficult situation. Global growth dynamics are sizable, and the rate of innovations is higher than ever. But at the same time, the worldwide situation concerning the environment, poverty and distribution issues, as well as the balance between cultures, becomes increasingly unsustainable. It was against this background that the Initiative for World Peace, Sustainability and Equity (www.initiative-weltfrieden.org) started the campaign **"Global Marshall Plan"**, which aims at changing this unfavorable situation. The reflections on the topic have been inspired by **Al Gore**'s "Earth in the Balance" [35], **Mikhail Gorbachev**'s "My Manifesto for the Earth" [34], **Hans Küng**'s "World Ethos" [62], the document "Crossing the Divide. Dialogue among Civilizations" initiated by **Kofi Annan** [3], and by the Earth Charter [117]. All of these comprehensive reflections and positions contain crucial points of orientation and organizing principles for the positioning of the Initiative for a Marshall Plan for the World.

In the Initiative's view, the already globalized economy has to be provided with an **adequate global organizing frame** for the markets, working towards World Peace, equity and sustainability and allowing for the realization of an **open society** [109]. Today, the contrary is the case. Our long-term perspective is an **Eco-Social World Market Economy** [87, 93] which links markets and competition to high standards ensuring the welfare of all human beings. Key to reaching a consensus on such standards - and at the same time, to overcome worldwide poverty - **are adequately framed co-financing measures** provided by the rich countries for the benefit of the poor. This requires that in return, the developing countries prove willing to adopt respective standards despite having to give up current competitive advantages. In particular better standards implicate **better governance** structures in these countries, i.e. improved local governance. The approach pursued here corresponds to the logic behind the **EU enlargement processes**, but also to that of the US Marshall Plan for Europe after World War II.

That a respective step is taken for the entire world is deemed urgent and long-overdue by the initiators of the campaign, especially with regard to the incidents of September 11, 2001, the obvious problems encountered by the current US policy, e.g. in Iraq, the devastations on global financial markets and the „Bubble" of the New Economy, the increasing environmental problems and the ever more apparent collision of cultures resulting from an **insufficiently regulated Globalization of the Economy**. The aim of the Initiative is that the EU convenes an advisory board after the EU parliamentary elections in summer 2004, due to develop a respective position the EU can adopt as its **strategy for future World Summits**, and as its vision for the future of the globe.

A Marshall Plan for the World is regarded as an intermediate step towards a worldwide Eco-Social Market Economy. The material goal currently pursued is the implementation of the **United Nations Millennium Development Goals** (www.un.org/millenniumgoals/) until 2015, which have gained broad international approval. The funding requirements are based on analysis by the United Nations (**Zedillo Report**, www.un.org/reports/financing/full_report.pdf), on the European position expressed by British Chancellor of the Exchequer **Gordon Brown** for the World Summit Rio+10 in Johannesburg 2002 [www.globalpolicy.org/socecon/ffd/2002/1216brown.htm], as well as on the analysis G. Soros provides in his pursuit of an open society (Open Society Initiatives, G. Soros, www.soros.org) [109]. According to these sources, additional aid amounting to US$ 980 billion will be needed until 2015, on top of the current volume of international development assistance. What is more, these funds would have to be employed through distinctly different mechanisms than today, and in close interaction with world civil society. By virtue of commitments already undertaken from 2006 onwards, this sum is reduced to about US$ 860 billion. Adequate regulatory conditions provided, and by concentrating initially on cooperative developing countries, from 2008 onwards the funds required per year could be raised by means of, e.g.:

- **Special Drawing Rights** of the International Monetary Fund, initially amounting to US$ 30 billion, then US$ 40 billion for the benefit of the developing countries.

- A worldwide tax on financial transactions (**Tobin tax**), initially amounting to 0.01 %, then 0.02 % of the traded value. This should result in annual funds of US$ 30 billion and 40 billion, respectively.

- A tax on international trade (**Terra tax**) of initially 0.35 %, then 0.5 % of cross-border value of goods within the scope of the WTO. Annual proceeds are expected to amount initially to US$ 30 billion, then to US$ 40 billion.

New forms of implementation are as important as the raising of funds [109]. To this end, the program uses the **World Bank** and the **United Nations Development Program** (UNDP), and cooperates with the UN environmental programs of the **UNEP** as well as with, e.g., **UNESCO** and the **United Nations Population Fund** (UNFPA). These should rely more on local initiatives and NGOs, support adjusted technologies and the accumulation of wealth on site. In addition, the allocation of co-financing measures of these organizations could be made subject to competitive processes where private development initiatives are chosen for funding under the control of an independent jury.

The **core standards of the ILO** [www.ilo.org/public/english/bureau/gender/newsite2002/standard/] and the **Global Environmental Agreements** should be made universally binding in the context of the WTO. This has been frequently demanded for the advancement of the WTO by the developed world, and especially the US; a demand corresponding in particular to the concerns of unions in the developed countries, and to worldwide concerns of environmentalists.

Starting from the aspired initiating step on the part of EU Parliament and EU Commission, the schedule of the Initiative aims at a process leading to a decision on an implementation program from 2008 onwards, to be made at the **Rio+15 conference** in 2007. Thus, the comprehensive considerations of the 1992 Earth Summit in Rio would then come into full effect.

The **design process for a Global Marshall Plan** presents a big challenge. This applies in particular to the new forms of implementing worldwide development cooperation, which are direly needed and a prerequisite for the Initiative's success. Respective ideas should now be developed in interaction between international organizations and governments, internationally operating corporations and non-governmental organizations. In this triangle, the **United Nations**, the **World Business Council on Sustainable Development** and the **Club of Rome** could assume an important coordinating role.

Detail information on the topic can be found at www.faw.uni-ulm.de and www.globalmarshallplan.org

Addendum 2

The Global Marshall Plan Initiative, presented to the public on October 11, 2003 as the Declaration of Stuttgart

A Global Marshall Plan for a worldwide Eco-Social Market Economy

Global Marshall Plan Initiative

Enabling a new form of economic miracle with a Global Marshall Plan for a worldwide eco-social market economy. After World War II, the United States of America decided to take a historical step: For the duration of four years, the US increased its budget for economic support measures directed at other countries to an average 1.3 % of its gross national product (against 0.1 % today). With this measure, the so called Marshall Plan for a haggard Europe, devastated by the war, was funded. The Marshall Plan made a decisive contribution to the European economic miracle, as well as to an exceedingly successful pacification both in- and outwardly, and to a broad-based increase of wealth in Europe.

Today, peace, freedom, prosperity and security are under threat, mainly due to extreme economical disparities. 50 percent of the world's population have to get by with less than two Euro per day, and 26,000 human beings a day die of starvation and lack of safe drinking water. Nor can the still mounting global environmental problems be solved without the prospect of a better world for all.

Our appeal today addresses mainly Europe to take the lead in a worldwide movement for a Global Marshall Plan. A Global Marshall Plan is capable of:

- Providing the most solid foundation for a new, sustainable worldwide economic upturn, as the catching up of less developed countries provides an enormous worldwide potential for economic growth, including decisive new impulses of demand for export countries.

- Opening a particularly intelligent and efficient way towards a worldwide development which is socially and ecologically sustainable: The example of the EU enlargement demonstrates the ecological, social, democratic and peace-making cycle that can be set in motion by linking co-financing for boosting economy to the enhancement of ecological, social and democratic standards in the receiving countries.

The successful European model of an Eco-Social market economy is reflected in the programs of most of the conservative, social-democratic, liberal or green parties in Europe, because it is a plausible concept which could serve as a standard for the framework of a new global cooperation. Without question, a European Initiative for a Global Marshall Plan to promote this success model worldwide would be a historical step capable of ensuring Europe's credit and success for decades to come.

Therefore, we demand that an advisory board of the European Union is convened for the development of an eco-social Global Marshall Plan.

The contents of such a Global Marshall Plan should be elaborated step by step and with strong involvement of all parts of society, including politics and economy, science and culture, as well as civil society. We consider the following points to be of particular importance:

- That the best ecological and social projects in the world are specially scrutinized together with Non-Governmental Organizations of global civil society, with the objective of massively increasing the efficiency of support programs for ecological and social change,

- That small and medium-sized companies and actors receive special support within the framework of this Global Marshall Plan.

- That those Non-Governmental-Organizations sustaining this Initiative are taken up on their offer to support such a Global Marshall Plan using their full potential.

We are determined to promote this Initiative for as long as it takes to accomplish the aspired objectives.

For further information: www.globalmarshallplan.org

Extract of Signatories of the Global Marshall Plan Initiative

as of June 25, 2004

Dr. Franz Alt, TV-Journalist, Author

Fernando Sanchez Arias, President Junior Chamber International

Dieter Althaus, Prime Minister of Thuringia

Josip Baotic, President Eco-Social Forum Croatia

Senta Berger, Actress

Dr. Vinod Bhalla, Businessman of the Year USA

Dr. Maritta von Bieberstein Koch-Weser, CEO GEXSI

HRH Prince El Hassan Bin Talal of Jordan, President Club of Rome

Carl-Eduard von Bismarck,
President Federal Ass. for Business Promotion and Foreign Trade (BWA)

Almaz and Karlheinz Böhm, Founder 'Menschen für Menschen'

René Böll, Artist, Publisher

Dr. Helga Breuninger, Director Breuninger Foundation

Dr. Fritz Brickwedde, President Deutsche Bundesstiftung Umwelt

Andreas Bummel, Managing Director Committee for a Democratic UN

Bert Christmann, President Junior Chamber Germany

Sir Arthur C. Clarke, Author

Prof. Paul J. Crutzen, Max-Planck Institute for Chemistry, Mainz

Borbála Czakó, President of Hungarian Business Leaders Forum

Ulrich Martin Drescher, Executive Board UnternehmensGrün

Prof. Dr. Eugen Drewermann, Theologian

Prof. Dr. Hans-Peter Dürr, Club of Rome, Alternative Nobel Prize Laureate

Dr. Peter Eigen, Chairperson Transparency International

Dr. Riane Eisler, Author

Prof. Dr. Duane Elgin, Futurologist

Count Hubertus von Faber-Castell, Entrepreneur

Peter Fernau, Member Board Club of Budapest

Lorenz Fritz, Secretary General Federation of Austrian Industry

Prof. Dr. Johann Galtung, Futurologist, Alternative Nobel Prize Laureate

Dr. Dietrich Garlichs, CEO UNICEF Germany

Prof. Dr. Maximilian Gege, Chairperson B.A.U.M.

Dr. Heiner Geißler, Former Federal Minister (Germany)

Hans-Dietrich Genscher, Former Foreign Minister (Germany)
Susan George, Transnational Institute, Amsterdam
Dr. Anselm Görres, Green Budget Germany
Rosi Gollmann, Founder Andheri Hilfe Bonn e.V., Germany
Dr. Friedemann Greiner, Director Protestant Academy Tutzing
Dieter Härthe, Federal Ass. for Business Promotion and Foreign Trade (BWA)
Dr. Berend Hartnagel, CEO Global Partnership
Dr. Volker Hauff, Chairman German Council for Sustainable Development
Dr. Bohan Hawrylyshyn, Club of Rome
Dr. Wolfgang Heidrich, EB Society for Promotion of Transfer and Innovation
Prof. Dr. Hazel Henderson, Economist, USA
Consul Peter Hesse, Peter Hesse Foundation
Prof. Vittorio Hösle, Professor of Philosophy, USA
Hans-Herbert Holzamer, Süddeutsche Zeitung
Wolfram Huncke, Journalist, Wuppertal Institute
Hans Jecklin, Entrepreneur, Author
Amod K. Kanth, Founder Children´s Fund Prayas, India
Prof. Dr. Margrit Kennedy, Futurologist
Marika Kilius, Former Olympic Champion in figure skating
Dr. Joachim Koch, Philosopher, Author
Wolfgang Kühr, Federal Ass. of Citizen Initiatives for Environmental Protection
Du´aine Ladejo, Former 400m European Champion
Prof. Dr. Dr. Ervin Laszlo, President Club of Budapest
Jo Leinen, MEP
Rainer von Leoprechting, EU Comission
Frauke Liesenborghs, Managing Director Global Challenges Network
Shu-hsien Liu, Chinese Philosopher
Dr. Reinhard Loske, Dep. Chairman, Parl. Party of the Greens, Germany
Franz Maier, Managing Director Umweltdachverband Austria
Sandra Maischberger, TV-Presenter
Prof. Dr. Ram Adhar Mall, Society of Intercultural Philosophy
Prof. Dr. Reinhard Malz, University of Applied Sciences, Esslingen
Reinhold Messner, Environmental activist
Dr. Paul E. Metz, Managing Consultant
Uwe Möller, Secretary General Club of Rome
Lady Fiona Montague, Ambassadress Club of Budapest International
Helga und Hans-Jürgen Müller, Project Mariposa

Karl-Heinrich Müller, Foundation Hombroich
Dr. Robert Muller, Former Vice Secretary General of the UN
Prof. Dr. Gyorgy Nógrádi, University of Economics, Budapest
Dr. Marcia Odell, Manager Women's Empowerment Program, Nepal
Dr. Ute-Henriette Ohoven, UNESCO Ambassadress
Christian Osterhaus, CEO 'Menschen für Menschen'
Rajendra K. Pachauri, Chairman of the IPCC
Siegfried Pater, Film-maker and Author
Maartje van Putten, Inspection Panel World Bank
Prof. Dr. Dr. Franz Josef Radermacher, Global Contract Foundation
Dipl.-Ing. Dr. h. c. Josef Riegler,
Former Vice Chancellor of Austria, Eco-Social Forum Europe
Wolfgang Riehn, Executive Board Yehudi-Menuhin-Foundation
Mary Robinson, Former UN High Commissioner for Human Rights
Bibi Russell, Fashion for Development, Bangladesh
Dr. Peter Russell, Author
Daniel R. Schaubacher, President of People to People Belgium
Dr. Dr. Hermann Scheer, German MP, Alternative Nobel Prize Laureate
Prof. Ernst Scheiber, CEO Eco-Social Forum Europe
Friedrich Schorlemmer, Theologian
Dr. Irmgard Schwaetzer, Former Minister of State, Germany
Karl-Ludwig Schweisfurth, Schweisfurth Foundation
Prof. Dr. Dr. h.c. Udo Simonis, Science Center Berlin
Peter Spiegel, Secretary General Club of Budapest
George Starcher, Consultant, Author
Prof. Dr. Rita Süssmuth, Former President of German Parliament
Jakob von Uexküll, World Future Council Initiative
Sir Peter Ustinov, UNICEF Ambassador †
Beate Weber, Lady Mayor Heidelberg, Germany
Prof. Hubert Weiger, Honorary President of the Bavarian Section BUND
Prof. Dr. Raoul Weiler, President EU-Chapter Club of Rome, Brussels
Hubert Weinzierl, Honorary President BUND
Prof. Dr. Ernst Ulrich von Weizsäcker, German MP, Club of Rome
Prof. Dr. Lutz Wicke, Former State Secretary
Anders Wijkman, MEP
Dr. Georg Winter, Entrepreneur, B.A.U.M. and INEM
Michael Zammit Cutajar, Former Executive Secretary UNFCCC

Organizations

AIESEC Germany
Club of Budapest
Committee for a Democratic UN
Deutsche Bundesstiftung Umwelt (DBU)
Eco-Social Forum Austria
Eco-Social Forum Croatia
Eco-Social Forum Europe
Environmental Protection Encouragement Agency (EPEA)
Fairness Foundation
Federal Association for Business Promotion and Foreign Trade (BWA)
German Association of the Junior Chamber International (WJD)
German Association for the Club of Rome
Global Contract Foundation
The United World Philharmonic Youth Orchestra
Umweltdachverband (Austria)
VENRO - Association of German Development NGOs
YOIS

This list only shows an extract of the supporters of the Global Marshall Plan Initiative. The complete list is available at http://www.globalmarshallplan.org. For further information: www.globalmarshallplan.org

Testimonials by Signatories

"This Initiative will help to reduce poverty in developing countries, and will enable them to adopt domestic policies and strengthen institutions that will empower people to take advantage of global markets and thus will sharply increase the share of trade in their GDP. Reducing the debt of the most marginalized countries, especially in Africa, will create opportunities for them to participate more actively in globalization and the benefits it can bring [...]. This will also create more opportunities such as debt relief, which is particularly powerful for those countries that improve their investment climate and social services - thus enhancing the HIPC Initiative effectively. Encouraging investment and creating jobs requires good economic governance - measures to eradicate corruption, better-functioning bureaucracies and better regulation, contract enforcement, and protection of property rights - which will lead to sustainable development, especially in developing nations. I regard the Global Marshall Plan Initiative as a fine integration towards sustainable development and advise other individuals, organizations, institutions, agencies [...] to seek to apply its principles in their formal and informal setting."
Mr. Akarue Careca Aghogho
CEO Liberty 4 Africa

"The realisation of the ecological Marshall Plan leads to a more just world, in which a child must no longer starve. That is our goal. Why shouldn't all industrial societies in the next decade achieve what the USA achieved in Western Europe after 1945 with the earlier Marshall Plan? The money is there - but the political will is still missing. Everyone and anyone can assist. Only then will the politics be dematerialised and human."
Franz Alt
TV Journalist and Author

"The relationships of nations today are generally presented as conflicts or battles, for example battles over work places or natural resources. I think that this account is misleading. The population must pull together much more in order to tackle the global problems. Global wealth can only be created when all people are in a position to implement an ecological and social economy as well as be able to make use of comprehensive education and the latest technology."
Thomas Bliem

Thinking back to Marshall's idea to rebuild Europe, the continent so atrociously destroyed through the dreadful Second World War and the crimes of Adolf Hitler and his collaborators, was not an act of mercy but simply the victors' wish to reinstall Europe as a creative commercial partner. This also lead to the introduction of the American economic system, the "debt principle".
The fact that Africa and other colonial nations need support for their development, should not solely be motivated by bad conscious but by the realistic consideration that without these countries - with a quarter of the world's population - without a doubt, there would be an economic disaster of unknown extent. One should not only think about the unimaginable poverty in these countries but especially about the future generations of our rich part of the world. That is the reason why I founded MENSCHEN FÜR MENSCHEN (people for people) and why I fully support ways of thought and action like that of a global economical plan."
Dr. h.c. Karlheinz Böhm
Founder of Menschen für Menschen

"The Breuninger Foundation is involved with international projects for adolescents to promote global awareness and action. These activities on the micro-level are just as important as the projects on the macro-level. I was convinced by the Global Marshall Plan Initiative's pragmatic approach. Only if we succeed to advance projects on the micro and macro level through

mutual support, will we reach the common goal: To make globalisation more just and ecologically acceptable, so that future generations will continue to have a future on this planet."
Dr. Helga Breuninger
CEO Breuninger Foundation

"Since the conference in Rio in 1992, the Deutsche Bundesstiftung Umwelt (German Federal Economic Foundation) has formally committed itself to the objectives of sustainability and adjusted its guidelines for funding accordingly. The alignment of its funding guidelines to cross-border and international funding can be seen in the foundation's overseas commitment for environmental protection and sustainability. A multitude of projects was supported in eastern Europe. The objectives of the Global Marshall Plan are in line with the orientation of the DBU. From the point of view of a foundation which focuses in its projects on small and medium-sized enterprises, we especially welcome the Initiative's cooperation with the private enterprise and the civil society considering fundamental entrepreneurial aspects to in tiate a "new worldwide economic miracle" which combines a cemocratic social order, the protection of the environment and fighting poverty."
Dr. Fritz Brickwedde
President DBU

"Manage in a way that your way of management can be a model for future generations': This is the direction we, as environmentally orientated entrepreneurs, try to follow, especially in the light of unequally distributed economic development chances on a global level."
Ulrich Martin Drescher
Founder of "UnternehmensGrün"Stuttgart

"Ecology is the Economy of the 21st Century! Until now, socio-ethic and ecological aspects of the progressing globalisation have been strongly neglected. Of special severity are the effects on the climate - something we have already started to

experience. This applies especially when industrialising countries, which are based on dated and environmentally destructing standards, experience a boom.
If we as human beings want to survive this century, we must now join forces globally and invest in a eco-social and sustainable market economy. Money is invested into innovations and projects. That also applies to private financial investment, which can be used to invest in sustainable economies."
Norbert Drews
eco-best-invest

"How to teach the Global Marshall Plan?
It is of utmost importance that one wins the hearts of the children and youths with this scheme, and that their enthusiasm is stimulated, since it is their world that we hope to be able to improve in the long run. If the aims of the Global Marshall Plan Initiative are explained properly to these young people in schools and universities, this encouragement can affect the whole human life.
In order to introduce the contents of the Global Marshall Plan Initiative into the educational systems of the various countries and to make the very complicated and extensive fields of knowledge understandable for young people learning for their future life, we will have to enter into strategic alliances. Essential aspects of the argumentation will have to be identified and adapted with help from the experts in that particular field of education. The aim is to create educational programmes (supported by internet, and in numerous languages) and to make the themes comprehensible for different age groups."
Edwin Ferger
Publishing House Ferger

"I support the "Global Marshall Plan Initiative" because we are desperately in need of visions and concrete concepts, for which we can all aim in our daily work. The Global Marshall Plan offers such a vision. Finding sustainable alternatives to the past and existing ways of globalization, are also the goals to which the World Future Council and B.A.U.M. are committed. Only when globalization is sustained, meaning eco-social, will we be able to achieve peace, freedom, security and wealth for all people. It is now essential to develop and implement concrete programs and concepts, which will make it possible to make these visions become a reality and to disperse them worldwide. There the "Global Marshall Plan Initiative" can make an important contribution."

Prof. Dr. Maximilian Gege
Executive board B.A.U.M. e.V.
Vice President World Future Council

"[...] that we carry responsibility in these times not only for ourselves, but for all future generations [...]. This example must apply without blinders to the problems. That is the major goal of the Stuttgart Declaration from today, which I support with all my heart, and I wish for everyone here to assimilate and contribute in spreading the word."

Hans-Dietrich Genscher
Former German Foreign Minister

"Already the consensus on the goals is not easy - but what is even harder is the consensus on the means. This became evident in the massive rejection of the German "Eco Tax reform", in particular through "petrol populists". At the same time it is clear: the goals of the Global Marshall Plan Initiative are demanding, likewise the goals from Kyoto. The only chance to realize these goals, lies in combining all reasonable and effective instruments. There is no room for infantile competition between the advocates of different instruments, like between the advocates of emission trading and the supporters of the "Eco Tax". It is also evident, that re-routing the economy towards global sustainability can only succeed when the huge steering power of the fiscal system is applied."

Dr. Anselm Görres
Chairman Green Budget Germany

"As founder of the German development organization Andheri-Hilfe Bonn e.V., I have been confronted for more than 40 years with the unacceptable injustice in this world. Close partnerships with the poor and oppressed, the disenfranchised and marginalized in addition to alarming experience on site, caused me to be one of the first to sign the the Stuttgart Declaration. The problem of inequality in our world is also a reason for violence, war and terrorism. We cannot accept that silently but instead must raise our voices for all the voiceless sufferers. Therefore for years I have worked intensively with the German group "Eine Welt für alle" and am Creative Member of the Club of Budapest. I am convinced that a new economic miracle can only be achieved when the poor, exploited and the unequal are integrated. For them but not without them! This must be an important principle in this new Initiative."
Rosi Gollmann
Founder Andheri-Hilfe, Bonn

"The Global Marshall Plan Initiative is a positive program to shift the world towards more equitable, ecologically-restorative, sustainable human development. Renewable energy and resource-based economies can replace today's disastrous competitive, resource-wasting globalization. More democratic, home-grown, locally-based economic prosperity can foster millions of new enterprises and hundreds of millions of new jobs and sustainable livelihoods. This strategy of a new information-rich "globalization" is technologically achievable today."
Prof. Dr. Hazel Henderson

"I support the Global Marshall Plan Initiative because current trends in world politics, economics, demography are simply not tenable. Unless fairly radical actions are undertaken on a global scale, humanity is heading towards a disaster. We need improvement in Global Governance, a return towards real multilateralism, significant help to less developed countries on condition of their commitment to adhere to political, administrative, environmental standards, reduction in growing gaps bet-

ween the rich and the poor within counties and between countries".
Dr. Bohdan Hawrylyshyn
Chairman International Center for Policy Studies
- Geneva/Kyiv

"For me, the idea was so easy and through that impressive: to transfer an idea that has already functioned well to today conditions and to ask for its support. As a child I also benefited from the Marshall Plan. Therefore I think it's only just if others - especially children, who are always affected the most - benefit from the new plan. We need to do something along these lines. I have therefore spontaneously decided to support the Global Marshall Plan Initiative as a complement to other initiatives such as Greenpeace."
Krzyzstof Jablonka

"I wish for a Europe that not only supports the United Nations Millennium Development Goals with words but also with deeds. To be precise: through further opening of markets for poorer countries but also through more public development aid. While working for the IMF, I saw hunger and inconceivable misery, especially with women and children. But I also saw that targeted development cooperation can do a lot of good. For me the humaneness of our world is linked with Africa's fate. Isn't it a question of Europe's self-respect, in the light of our own foundations, values and history, to show honest and generous involvement in Africa?"
Horst Köhler
Excerpt from his inaugural speech as Federal President on 1 July 2004 in the German Bundestag (www.bundespraesident.de)

"The Global Marshall Plan represents for me the most convincible and realistic sustainability concept, that can, in the long run, help to overcome worldwide social injustice. With the

implementation of this plan, Europe would have the unique chance to put a world peace mission into effect.
I support this Initiative with all my heart and inner fire, because it has the welfare of all people in this imperilled planet in mind."
Dr. Manfred Kohlhase
Ecomanager 2002

"I support the Global Marshall Plan Initiative because it aims at imbedding the global markets in a social and ecological frame of order from the local to the global level and at strengthening the roll of the civil society against the fast developing economy. At the same time, the ecology must not be neglected: There can not be combat against poverty in the South without environmental protection, and there will also be no global wealth without a reduction in the use of resources in the north."
Dr. Reinhard Loske
Deputy Chairman of the parliamentary party of the Greens, Germany

"Global Marshall Plan: From Words to Actions! The Global Marshall Plan Initiative is one of the most promising European movements for the necessary step-by-step transformation of our economic, financial and political system towards sustainability. No utopias or ideologies are proclaimed, but feasible, efficient, and effective ways for a worldwide Eco-Social market economy. For me it is the attempt to shake off the ties of the ancients, "saturated" Europe, to overcome the bureaucratic, budgetary and political hurdles, as well as to venture a new start to more peace, wealth and security on this planet. As an environmentalist I am especially concerned about securing biodiversity and the basis for natural foundations of life. The Global Marshall Plan Initiative is the great chance to walk the talk of the many conferences and papers."
Franz Maier
Director Umweltdachverband (Austria)

"The world is in a complex crisis on many fields. The main scarcity is Good Governance to manage this situation and prevent increasing chaos. I believe that the Global Marshall Plan Initiative is a constructive force for the promotion of Good Governance by integrating sustainable development into the proces of globalization - which is usually believed to be autonomous, unstoppable and uncontrolable. It is not, and it can be made humane and more productive by creating a high-level playing field of social, ecological and cultural qualities."
Dr. Paul E. Metz
Managing Consultant INTEGeR consult

"I consider the idea to promote a Global Marshall Plan excellent and exemplary, for such an Initiative would point out to people in the developing and swelling countries and in war-torn and dangerous regions the way out of the crisis, which would promise a humane and self determined life. We in Europe know exactly what we are talking about, for it was the Marshall Plan which proved a way out for us after the catastrophe of the second World War from ruins, sorrow, tyranny, terror and fear. Without the Marshall Plan, the democracies which were rebuilt in Europe after the war would have remained an unrealised dream."
Dr. Ute-Henriette Ohoven
UNESCO Ambassadress

"The Global Marshall Plan commemorates the fact, that instead of "small strategies", "big" comprising strategies were also possible when it was about showing solidarity to overcome the consequences of the second World War. For 50 years, the community of states has not seized the opportunity of an Initiative comparable to the Marshall Plan. When, if not now, is such an opportunity offered - an opportunity to combat the causes and consequences of the World Wars against the natural basis of life?"
Dr. Dr. Hermann Scheer
MP Germany, Alternative Nobel Prize laureate

"The Marshall Plan was a visionary plan. The same kind of visionary plan is needed today, not to rebuild once-prosperous countries and economies, but to bring prosperity, economic development, and democratic government to places and peoples who have been denied them too long."

Jürgen E. Schrempp
Chairman Daimler Chrysler

"In the process of globalization with striking concomitant differences in the development of different regions in the world, the increasing global interdependence must be made public and shaped also with urgent global challenges and questions of peace, security, demographic change, use of resources, protection of the environment etc. It has to be recognized that economic development furthers the set-up of social standards and consequently peace and (international) security - conditions which, among other things, make less people flee and migrate from their homelands. This list of examples for such dependencies could be enlarged endlessly. It is most important that these dependencies are recognised and that it is understood that the sole concentration on national solutions will not solve global problems. Goals and insights of the developed countries shall not lead to the exclusion of the developing countries from global wealth but must contribute to their development.

It is important that we create general conditions, in which the numerous challenges of today's world are addressed and are tackled by us as stakeholders. For that, the various actors such as NGOs, governments, institutions and other initiatives must jointly develop and discuss corresponding strategies.

Coordinated economic development aid helps to share the positive effects of globalization as well as the responsibility for upcoming global problems with all countries and regions of the world."

Prof. Dr. Rita Süssmuth
Former President of German Parliament

"The future is most important. For me as a singer, composer and producer (The Globalization Saga - Balance or Destruction) that has become the life motto. Globalization, migration, ecology and electric power are issues with which every person, independent from work and vocation, should be concerned. Therefore I support the Global Marshall Plan Initiative; because we all live in this world and need initiatives like this. When we understand this and act accordingly, life on this planet will be a wonderful never-ending story for us and future generations."
Solvig Wehsener
Singer / Composer

"I think that your Initiative harbours one of the greater hopes for humanity in this critical period."
M. Willemse Stichting
Voedselbank Noord-Limburg

"What is really remarkable in the Global Marshall Plan Initiative is the visible positive action and stable development step by step! The famous Russian academic Nikita Moiseev (1917 - 2000) wrote in 1996 about the necessity of the New Marshall Plan. I quite agree with Professor Radermacher: a "business as usual" approach can not be ecologically endured beyond some kind of limited irreversible process because it will bring our planet to a state of global catastrophe the responsibility of our generation is to stop and to convert destructive trends and to support positive action!"
Dr. Vladimir Zolotarev
Noosphere Information Fund (Global Survival)

The Author

Franz Josef Radermacher, born in 1950, married, 1 son. Holds a PhD in mathematics and economics (RWTH Aachen 1974, University of Karlsruhe 1976). Postdoctoral lecture qualification in mathematics from the RWTH Aachen in 1982. 1983-1987 professor for applied information technology at the University of Passau. Since 1987 director of the Research Institute for Applied Knowledge Processing (FAW) in Ulm. At the same time appointed professor for data bases and artificial intelligence at the University of Ulm. 1988-1992 president of the Society for Mathematics, Economy and Operations Research (GMÖOR). 1990-1993 member of the research council of Baden-Wuerttemberg, 1992-1993 member of the "Future Commission Economy 2000", 1994-1996 member of the "Innovation Council" and 1995-1996 member of the Enquête Commission "Development Chances and Effects of new Information and Communication Technologies Baden-Wuerttemberg (Multimedia Enquête)".

Since 1995 member of the "Information Society Forum" of the European Commission (since beginning of 1997 also director of the working group for "Sustainability in an Information Society" as well as member of the steering committee). Since 1997 spokesperson of the working group "Information Society and Sustainable Development" in the Forum Info 2000 / Forum Information Society of the German Federal Government. 1997 laureate of the Science Prize of the Society for Mathematics, Economy and Operations Research (GMÖOR). 1997 member of the scientific council of the EXPO 2000 AG for the subject areas "Planet of Visions" and "The 21st Century". Since 2000 member of the scientific council of the Federal Ministry of Transport, Civil Engineering and Housing (BMVBW). Since 2000 chairperson of the "Global Society Dialogue" of the Information Society Forum of the EU.

Since 2001 Vice President of the Eco-Social Forum Europe. Since 2002 member of the "Council for Sustainable Development" of the government of Baden-Wuerttemberg as well as member of the jury for the nomination for the German Environmental Award. 2002 member of the "Train Council" of the Deutsche Bahn AG.

2002 member of the Club of Rome. Since 2002 member of the board of trustees of the Global Contract Foundation. 2003 appointed to the council of "art, science & business" of the Academy Schloss Solitude, Stuttgart. 2003 President of the scientific council of the Federal Association for Business Promotion and Foreign Trade (BWA). Member of the German National Committee of the UNESCO for the world decade "education for sustainable development " 2005 – 2014.

2003 appointed scientific coordinator of the Global Marshall Plan Initiative.

Prof. Radermacher is the author of more than 200 scientific papers in the areas of applied mathematics, operations research, applied information technology, systems theory as well as related issues of research of the consequences of technology and ethics / philosophy; the latter also in relation with global problems. His sociopolitical interest is focused on the changeover to the information society, learning organizations, treatment of risks, responsibility of individuals and systems, environmentally friendly mobility, sustainable development and the problem of excess of population.

The Research Institute for Applied Knowledge Processing (FAW) is a foundation under public law with the following founders: State of Baden-Wuerttemberg, Compaq Computer GmbH, DaimlerChrysler AG, Deutscher Sparkassen Verlag GmbH, Jenoptik AG, State of Carinthia, Robert Bosch GmbH, Stadtsparkasse Cologne, Tecomac AG and ZF Friedrichshafen AG. The institute develops integrated systemic solutions in information technologically demanding interdisciplinary subject areas, especially integrated production systems, enterprise integration, decision supporting systems, environmental information systems, assisting systems, transport, communication systems, industrial software production, autonomous systems, mechatronics; here the development of the environmental information system of Baden-Wuerttemberg is scientifically accompanied.

More publications of the same author

Radermacher, F. J.:
Balance or Destruction: Eco-Social Market Economy as key to worldwide sustainable Development.
Eco-Social Forum Europe, Vienna 2002

Price: 15,- Euro
To be ordered at www.globalmarshallplan.org (in German or English)

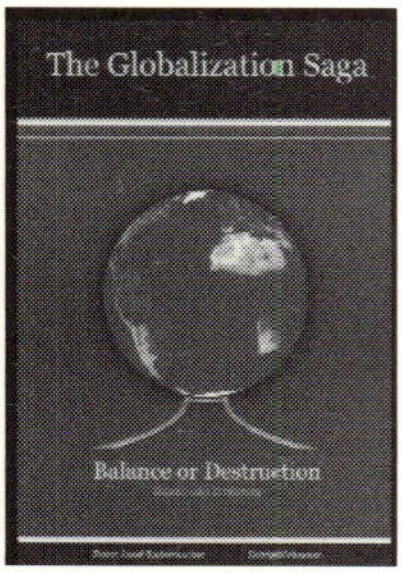

Radermacher, F. J. and Wehsener, S.:
The Globalization Saga - Balance or Destruction. Musical Storybook, CD and VHS Video. Ulm, 2003/2004

Individual Price: 15,- Euro
Two Parts: 25,- Euro
All Parts: 35,- Euro

To be ordered at www.globalmarshallplan.org (in German or English)